Sarum Chronicle

recent historical research on Salisbury & district

Issue 12: 2012

Contents

Editorial

We are delighted to announce that *Sarum Chronicle* 11, the first edition produced under our new self-financing regime, has proved a great success. This was due to much hard work from all members of the Editorial Team, and to the enthusiasm of our readers. We have attracted a number of new subscribers, several of whom also purchased sets of the first 10 issues (still available, please see below for details) and have expanded the number of local outlets stocking *Sarum Chronicle*.

The official launch of our new look publication took place on Wednesday 23 November 2011 at Sarum College, when a packed audience heard John Chandler's talk on Salisbury St Thomas's medieval doom painting. It is published here as our lead article entitled 'The Damned Bishop'. We hope that a *Sarum Chronicle* lecture will become an annual event with a version of the talk appearing in the following year's issue.

Sarum Chronicle 12 also contains a collection of articles that covers diverse topics and a wide time period, from authors of very varying backgrounds. It is exciting to be able to reflect the vibrancy of local history work in the district.

As ever we need your support to ensure our future existence – so please contact us if you have a piece of research on the Salisbury area which would make a suitable article, tell your friends about us and encourage them to buy a copy.

How to contact us:

To order a copy of the current edition phone Ruth Newman on 01722 328922 or email ruth.tanglewood@btinternet.com

Copies of issues 1-10 are available at the price of £3 per copy, or £25 for the set, plus postage at cost. Please contact Jane Howells on 01722 331426 or email as below.

To submit material for consideration in future editions e-mail Jane Howells at jane@sarum-editorial.co.uk with the words Sarum Chronicle in the subject line.

Editorial Team: John Chandler, John Elliott, Jane Howells, Sue Johnson, Ruth Newman, David Richards and Margaret Smith.

The Damned Bishop

John Chandler

Few things in Salisbury better illustrate the old cliché, 'every picture tells a story', than the so-called doom painting in St Thomas's church, and more particularly its portrayal of a bishop about to be dragged down to hell.[1] It has long fascinated me. Nearly 30 years ago I wrote of the picture as 'a medieval guidebook to heaven and hell' and quoted Albert Hollaender, who described it as a 'permanently-exposed lantern slide'.[2] Hollaender was a brilliant Austrian journalist and scholarly art historian who escaped to England in 1938, learnt English, catalogued Salisbury's manuscripts and became a distinguished archivist.[3] In 1944 he wrote a paper about the painting which must be the starting-point for any further research.[4] My concern is not so much with the painting itself, as to try to understand what it, and the bishop especially, may have to tell us about the society that created them.

First, some facts and figures. Medieval doom paintings illustrate passages in St Matthew's gospel, chapters 24 and 25, which were later rendered into English thus:

> And he shall send his angels with a great sound of a trumpet, and they shall gather together his elect from the four winds, from one end of heaven to the other . . . When the son of man shall come in his glory, and all the holy angels with him, then shall he sit upon the throne of his glory; and before him shall be gathered all nations: and he shall separate them one from another, as a shepherd divideth his sheep from the goats. And he shall set the sheep on the right hand and the goats on the left. Then shall the King say unto them on his right hand, come, ye blessed of my father, inherit the kingdom prepared for you from the foundation of the world . . . Then shall he say also unto them on the left hand, Depart from me, ye cursed, into everlasting fire, prepared for the devil and his angels . . . and these shall go away into everlasting punishment; but the righteous into life eternal.[5]

They probably once adorned many, even most, churches, and were usually painted

The Devil (note the faces on his knees).
Courtesy of Alan Impey

on the east wall of the nave, above and around the chancel arch – as at Salisbury – at precisely the point where this sinful world, the nave of the laity, translated into the holy world, the sanctuary reserved for the priest.[6] Almost two-thirds (117) of the 182 recorded English dooms are here. Some are quite early, such as the 'ladder of Salvation' of about 1200, from Chaldon in Surrey,[7] but a large proportion – over 60 – date from the 15th or early 16th century, including the Salisbury doom. Here at Salisbury the proceedings are set out as a court of law, with the apostles as jury, Christ as judge, and opposing advocates the devil and St Peter (mistakenly repainted as an angel). The painting is full of vivid details and some, such as the faces painted on the devil's knees, are only visible with binoculars (to adapt a dictum – the detail is in the devil). The last judgement does show up in other media, too, as in the spectacular early Tudor west window at Fairford in Gloucestershire.[8] But unlike images and glass, which the iconoclasts destroyed at the Reformation, wall paintings were easily concealed beneath a layer of whitewash. Many more, therefore, may await discovery and restoration.

The survival rates are higher in the south-east and East Anglia than elsewhere in England, perhaps reflecting where antiquarian interest in them was most concentrated.[9] The history of Salisbury's is fairly typical.[10] Discovered in 1819, and then drawn by

Elizabeth Wickens (from which we see that no angel was visible opposite the devil),[11] before being covered over again, it was revealed once more in 1880 and restored in a way which would not now be acceptable, with further treatment in the 20th century. In the medieval Salisbury diocese survivors are quite rare, three in Wiltshire (Dauntsey, Winterslow (which survives only as a picture recording it) and Salisbury St Thomas, two in Berkshire (Ashampstead and Stanford Dingley), none in Dorset. There are also records of up to nine possible or suspected dooms. Locally the Winterslow doom was destroyed when the church was restored in 1851, but a lithograph as it appeared at the time is in the Wiltshire Heritage Museum, Devizes, and was published in 1909 – a crowned figure is among the damned.[12] And writing in 1837 the discursive antiquary Edward Duke mentioned a curious picture of the Last Day to be seen on the walls of Combe Church near Salisbury – presumably Coombe Bissett.[13] This too has vanished. A number of paintings known to or discovered thus by the Victorians were subsequently destroyed or concealed on purpose, as too crude and vulgar to be displayed in the house of God. The image, for example, of a smiling naked woman encouraging a devil to fondle her breast (at Combe in Oxfordshire) was not every vicar's cup of tea.[14] Most

The bishop in chains, with his unholy alliance. Courtesy of Alan Impey

Drawing by Elizabeth Wickens of the painting as uncovered in 1819, engraved for Hatcher's history of Salisbury, published in 1843

would have felt more comfortable with the sumptuous Arts and Crafts rendering, by Gambier Parry at Highnam near Gloucester – all wings and halos, and the cursed seem to have departed by a side door.[15]

Every part of the Salisbury doom repays inquisitive study, but surely the most interesting zone depicts the characters on their way to hell. The bishop is one of a group chained together, which includes a king and a queen, and probably (from his headgear) a judge.[16] Nearby are the figures of an alewife and a miser. A fairly obvious interpretation is therefore that people of all ranks will be damned, or that rank counts for nothing on the day of judgement. At Holy Trinity, Coventry, where a much disfigured doom painting was carefully restored between 1995 and 2003, this is clearly the message – two groups are balanced, one on either side of Christ's feet, and both include a king, queen, cardinal and pope.[17] Salisbury's in fact is not the only 'damned' bishop.[18] At Enfield (Middlesex) the doom painted on wooden boards has a pope, bishop and cardinal all being poked into hell by a demon with a stick. A chained group of the damned at North Leigh (Oxon) includes crowned, mitred and tonsured figures, and a now destroyed painting at Poslingford (Suffolk) had crowned and mitred figures. At South Leigh (Oxon) there are two kings, a queen, a tonsured priest, a cardinal, and a bishop who is having his mitre removed by a devil. Taken altogether, an analysis of doom paintings in 1980 (which did not include Coventry) found 20 churchmen on their way down, as it were, against 35 on their way up – but this could of course be a far from representative sample of what once existed.

At Salisbury, therefore, and these other examples, there seems to be a rather more pointed message aimed at those in authority, along the lines of, 'you can tell a man by the company he keeps'. Corrupt, idle and sinful churchmen in the 15th century were denounced from the pulpit by reforming preachers and in popular literature – Langland's parson 'Sleuth' in Piers Plowman, or Chaucer's Pardoner, who preached *Radix malorum est cupiditas* 'Greed is the root of evils' while passing round the collection plate.[19] There was truth in it too, and locally within Salisbury diocese.[20] On three occasions between 1405 and 1412 the dean of Salisbury held visitations of the 50 or so parishes which fell within his peculiar jurisdiction to find out what was going on, and to hear and adjudge complaints. Allegations of misconduct were heard against about one-quarter of the clergy, and there were some spectacular performers. The rector of Over Compton near Sherborne in 1405 was usually disgracefully drunk – he sometimes took services too quickly and sometimes too slowly. Alexander Champion, vicar of Burbage, was alleged in 1412 to have committed adultery with four parishioners' wives, one for the past seven years, had fathered many children by a mistress in Salisbury, and solicited wives and servant girls during confession. Maurice Tyler, rector of Caundle Marsh in north Dorset, was said to be drunk daily, neglected to take services, pawned church property, disparaged his parishioners and made trouble between them, neglected the church fabric, placed his ale jars on the altar, pretended that he could make holy oil (only a bishop could do that), and committed immorality with a servant girl and a woman from Yeovil. If the charges against him were true, he had probably managed to commit five of the seven deadly sins – sloth, gluttony, wrath, lust and avarice – leaving only pride and envy unaccounted for.

Mention of the seven deadly sins leads one to consider the company our bishop is keeping. At the Guild Chapel in Stratford on Avon the sins are personified, on one side, and contrasted with their counterpart, the seven acts of mercy, on the other.[21] At Salisbury the bishop's group is flanked by the miser or usurer with his moneybags, a stock figure from contemporary mystery plays representing avarice, and by the alewife. Alewives, literally, encompassed a multitude of sins. They cheated with short measures, they encouraged idleness and over indulgence, they tempted with their low-cut dresses, and they showed off their wealth with competing finery.[22] They feature on many doom paintings, often giving their tormentors the glad eye, as if looking forward

The alewife, dragged down by a demon. Courtesy of Alan Impey

to a diabolical party. And like the miser, the alewife is a regular character from mystery plays, a figure of derision, a pantomime dame.

There are other links, too, between doom paintings and medieval drama. Several hell mouths, including the one at Dauntsey in north Wiltshire, appear to be hinged, as if modelled on a stage set – and there are documentary references to building a hell mouth with a nether chap for a play at Lincoln, and in France to two large bolts for making hell mouth open.[23] At Oddington near Stow on the Wold (Glos) there is a graphic doom painting which includes a condemned king, and beside it another painting which has been identified as portraying all the characters from John Skelton's morality play, *Magnificence*.[24] And coming closer to home, has no-one ever noticed the resemblance between Christ and the Devil on the painting and the best known relic of Salisbury's medieval and Tudor pageantry? Guild processions are recorded from the 1440s and, although the Giant and Hobnob are not recorded until more than a century later, the wording suggests that they were then of some antiquity. The line-up is suggestive: 'the accustomed pageant of midsummer feast, the giant, the three black boys, the bearer of the giant and one person to play the devil's part' – in other words, Hobnob is a portrayal of the devil.[25]

The Salisbury doom, therefore, conformed to a pattern, which included not only the predictable elements of New Testament scripture, but also subversive criticism of the wielders and abusers of power, especially church leaders (hence the bishop), and a strong whiff of medieval greasepaint. But – like a village performance of *Cinderella* – alongside the conventional plot there are usually veiled references to the foibles and peccadilloes of local people, which those in the know will spot and enjoy. John Edwards, who identified the Oddington painting as *Magnificence*, went on to note that Skelton's play is thought to be a satire against Cardinal Wolsey – who, as chance would have it, was also absentee lord of the manor of Oddington (and therefore the recipient of the parishioners' rents).[26] Such an exalted personage never visited this remote Cotswold parish, so in this instance the satirist could mock with impunity. But maybe local circumstances of the later 15th century can be identified also in the Salisbury doom painting? There are a number of overlapping and interlocking possibilities, to which attention should now turn.

First there are two events which occurred a year apart, in June 1448 and June 1449. By a strange coincidence, what is known of them is noted on the front and back of the same piece of damaged vellum, at the beginning of a chapter act book preserved among the cathedral archives.[27] On the *recto* a meeting and agreement of June 1448 are noted, between the Dean and Chapter on the one hand, and a group of leading citizens and parishioners, including William Swayne, John a Port, William Lightfoot and John Halle, on the other. The chancel of St Thomas's and part of an adjoining chapel had recently collapsed, and the citizens saw an opportunity to rebuild the church on a larger and grander scale. But the rectory, and therefore responsibility for the chancel, belonged to the Dean and Chapter, and they were only prepared to rebuild to the same dimensions as the previous chancel. The citizens, grudgingly perhaps, compromised by agreeing themselves to pay for the extra 20ft of chancel they wanted.[28] This they did, as is proclaimed by the merchants' marks and inscription to John Nichol and his wife on the relevant columns. Those words, 'the founder of the peler wt [with] a part of the arche', should be read as a political statement: 'we are doing this in spite of the church authorities because for all their wealth they won't take their responsibilities seriously'. Of course this 1448 meeting is directly relevant to the damned bishop, at one level at least, because the wall on which he is painted was reconstructed as part of the new building work.

On the *verso*, written a year later in June 1449, is a note – now barely legible but transcribed (probably by Canon Wordsworth *c*1900) in the margin – about a serious riot staged by Salisbury citizens against Lord Moleyns at the George Inn. The Precentor and another canon intervened, by fetching 'the body of our lord' (the sacrament or eucharist) and using it as a talisman to quell the riot and lead the unfortunate Moleyns back into the Close and so to safety.[29] Moleyns was Robert Hungerford, a leading Wiltshire landowner and magistrate, and also an intimate at the court of the deeply unpopular king, Henry VI.[30] His rescuer, the Precentor, was Nicholas Upton, another of the courtiers who, 'were popularly blamed for social injustices and the disastrous war effort in France'. Upton had his own drama. Six months earlier, at Christmas 1448, one of the vicars choral in the Close had killed a canon's servant in a brawl after the boy bishop ceremony. In trying to prevent a recurrence the following Christmas Upton restricted the choristers' choice of boy bishop, but was then overruled by the Chapter, who seem to have feared that his action might spark a popular revolt in the city against them.[31]

Their fears were genuine – a few weeks later the former dean of Salisbury, by then bishop of Chichester, was killed by sailors at Portsmouth, and in June 1450, at the height of Jack Cade's rebellion, the bishop of Salisbury himself, William Ayscough, was lynched at Edington by a mob which included ringleaders from Salisbury. Much hated for his close association with Henry VI (he was described as one of the king's evil councillors), he seems to have borne the brunt of the anger in his diocese at weak government mismanagement, which was harming the local textile trade.[32] In Salisbury a few years earlier he had provoked a riot by asserting an ancient right to the tenure of some property bequeathed to the corporation.[33] He was in fact fleeing for his life when the mob caught him. Is he the bishop on the doom, inseparably bound to King Henry VI and his queen, Margaret of Anjou, over whose wedding he had presided, and to Lord

Moleyns the magistrate? Perhaps, although most authorities date the doom painting to the 1480s or 1490s, by when the murdered bishop would be remembered only by the old, and would have receded into folklore.

Perhaps one should delve rather inside the medieval church, and into its dilemma of beliefs. Albert Hollaender, when he studied the Salisbury doom in the 1940s, believed that the presence of the damned bishop was a theological statement, an expression of the reforming doctrines of John Wyclif which became known as Lollardy.[34] Wyclif was scathing of the feigned contemplative life of priests and blamed the Sarum Use for 'proud prestis, coveitous and dronkelewe'.[35] Although he had been dead for a century when the painting was made, his teachings survived as significant undercurrents in the life of the church right up to the Reformation — which in some senses they prefigured. Lollardy was supposed to have begun in Salisbury diocese, and the evidence — mostly circumstantial — has been assembled for its survival through the 15th century.[36] In 1475 there was a round-up of so-called heretics, and at least three, presumably found guilty of Lollardy, were burnt at the stake in Salisbury market place.

Central to Wyclif's teaching was the doctrine of dominion. Dominion (authority) rested with God, and could only be transmitted to those humans who were not sinful. But civil dominion was inherently sinful, and so the church should distance itself from it. Bishops who consorted with secular powers were condemned, and the church when it behaved as a civil power had fallen into sin. A bishop, king, queen and judge shackled together as they awaited the fires of hell would seem to embody this doctrine — and so, the argument runs, the painting is a not overly subtle Lollard message to the churchmen who resided at the other end of the High Street. It was a two-dimensional revenge, perhaps, by those who had actually seen their friends burnt by the secular and religious authorities for sincerely held beliefs.

A third possibility reflects the world of contemporary local politics.[37] As already noted, the 1448 meeting with the dean and chapter over the rebuilding of St Thomas's was attended by the leading Salisbury citizens. Two of these were old enemies, William Swayne and John Halle, who were prone to stand-up rows at council meetings. (There is a note in the city ledger that anyone using improper language at a meeting should be fined 3s 4d, but for Hall and Swayne the fine was £1 (first offence), £2 (second), gaol (third).)[38] These two became embroiled in a protracted and bitter dispute, not only with each other, but also with Bishop Ayscough's successor, Richard Beauchamp, who held on to the see until his death in 1481. As part of the reconstruction Swayne wished to build a chantry house on land adjacent to the church, so in 1465 he obtained the bishop's permission (as lord of the city) to do so and had built up as far as the chimneys. The land in question, however, had for nearly 30 years been claimed with some justification as council property, and council officers broke in by night and took possession. The bishop prosecuted the mayor and council – in the county court, not the city, where John Halle was one of the magistrates – and won. The council retaliated by expelling William Swayne from their number, and appealing to higher authority, the king. The bishop in person, and John Halle representing the city, were summoned to the king's council and, although the bishop behaved 'right soberly, discretely and to the peace therefore right conformably', John Halle 'of the old rancour and malice which he hath borne towards the said Reverende fader, as it should seem, brake out of the said mater, concernying the said citie, into his own matters.' He was slapped into gaol for contempt and the city was ordered to elect a new mayor, 'of sad, sober and discrete disposicion'. But the city stood by Halle and refused to replace him, in open defiance to the king.

This was the flashpoint of a controversy which rumbled on for nearly a decade. Underlying it was not just Halle's defiance, but the resentment of most of the leading citizens' at Bishop Beauchamp's intransigent and heavy-handed attitude towards them, as they saw it, and their wish for emancipation from his governance. At a personal level it was the bitterness most of the leading citizens felt for William Swayne, who had sided with the bishop against them. So how is this reflected in St Thomas's church? The south chapel was rebuilt as a chantry for William Swayne and his family, at his expense, and it was staffed by the chantry priests whom he had proposed to house in the building on land they felt he had misappropriated from the city. It has wall paintings very different

Wall paintings on the north arcade wall of the Swayne chantry chapel, depicting vignettes of Mary on a background of lilies and garter badges

The miser, dragged down by a demon (note the mark on his moneybag). Courtesy of Alan Impey

in character from the doom, vignettes of the annunciation, adoration and visitation, on a background painted to look like a curtain adorned with lilies and garter badges. Bishop Beauchamp, Swayne's supporter, was appointed chancellor of the order of the garter in 1475, and this seems therefore to be a tribute to him.[39]

Could it be that the doom painting is John Halle's revenge, his chance to pillory, for everyone to see, his enemy Bishop Beauchamp, and the king (Edward IV) who threw him into gaol? And what of that symbol on the miser's moneybag (which one needs a long lens to see) – could it once have been a merchant's mark, William Swayne's, even? Conceivably the painting is full of contemporary allusions of similar kind about which little or nothing can now be established – minor details such as the portcullis and battlements on one of the entrances to heaven. It is known for instance that for his own security Bishop Beauchamp added a portcullis to the High Street gate into the Close, and built battlements on his new work at the bishop's palace.[40]

It is an appealing prospect, even if the controversy had died down and the protagonists themselves had gone by the time the painting was finished. Halle died in 1479 and Beauchamp in 1481.[41] But the ill-feeling must have remained. The city, in its dispute with the bishop, had been cowed into submission by successive kings, but here in their church at least, which they had rebuilt at their own expense, they could vent their scorn of authority. And, as if to rub it in, when Beauchamp's successor was appointed at the beginning of 1482, he — Lionel Woodville — turned out to have the closest ties, of kinship, to royalty. He was the king's, Edward IV's, brother-in-law, and the queen, Elizabeth Woodville, was his sister.[42] They did not last long. Edward died the following year, and his sons — the princes in the tower — were murdered. Edward's last mistress (of many), Jane Shore, was made to do penance and then imprisoned by the new king, Richard III, who also confiscated the bishop's estates, suspecting him of treason. The bishop fled his see, and died in 1484.

So who is the damned bishop? This paper has suggested several possibilities — Ayscough, Beauchamp, Woodville, or an undefined but corrupt churchman. The fascination of looking at works of art is that there is no single interpretation, now or in the past. It depends on the viewer's response. Everyone involved with the creation of this painting has been dead for five centuries. No doubt at the time some saw Ayscough, some Beauchamp, some other bishops before and since; some were terrified by the cataclysmic events depicted, and others amused at the Punch-and-Judy style figures. What is certain, as is true of all great paintings, is that it generates the question and demands the response.

John Chandler is Editor of the Gloucestershire Victoria County History, but most of his long local history career has been concerned with Salisbury and Wiltshire, about which he has written, lectured and published extensively.

Bibliography & Abbreviations

VCH = Victoria County History
WANHM = Wiltshire Archaeological and Natural History Society Magazine

Ashby, J E, 1980, English medieval murals of the doom: a descriptive catalogue and introduction, M Phil thesis, University of York
Edwards, J, 1986, The mural and the morality play: a suggested source for a wall-

painting at Oddington, *Transactions of the Bristol & Gloucestershire Archaeological Society*, vol 104, 187-200

Haskins, C, 1912, *Ancient Trade Guilds and Companies of Salisbury*, Bennett Bros

Hollaender, A, 1944, The doom painting of St Thomas of Canterbury, Salisbury, *WANHM* vol 50, 351-70

Rosewell, R, 2008, *Medieval wall paintings in English and Welsh churches*, Boydell and Brewer

Street, F, 1915-17, Relations of the Bishops and Citizens of Salisbury . . ., *WANHM* vol 39, 185-257, 319-367

Tatton Brown, T, 1997, The church of St Thomas of Canterbury, Salisbury, *WANHM* vol 90, 101-9

Notes

1   This paper is a revised version of a lecture given in November 2011 at Sarum College, and in February 2012 in St Thomas's Church. I am grateful to those attending for their insights during questions and discussions. I am also most grateful to Alan Impey for making available to me his late wife's thesis, and for permitting reproduction of photographs taken for that thesis; and to Roger Rosewell and Dr Ellie Pridgeon for reading a draft of this paper, for their general comments, and for casting doubts on the interpretation of the Oddington painting. I have retained my reference to it as denoting a morality play in my text but with a caveat in note 24, pending their further research.

2   Chandler, J, 1983, *Endless Street*, 195; citing *WANHM* vol 50 (1944), 352

3   Ranger, F, 1973, *Prisca Munimenta: studies in archival and administrative history presented to A E J Hollaender*; Rathbone, M G, 1951, *List of Wiltshire Borough Records earlier in date than 1836* (WANHS Records Branch 5), xii, 63-85

4   Hollaender, A, 1944

5   St Matthew ch 24, 31; ch 25, 31-4, 41, 46 (Authorised Version)

6   The fullest treatment is by Ashby. The Salisbury doom is discussed on 343-7

7   Rosewell 73, 294

8   Brown, S and Macdonald, L, 1997, *Life, death and art: the medieval stained glass of Fairford church*

9   Ashby, 21-4

10   The fullest description of the Salisbury Doom is Impey, J M, 2009, *The Iconography of the Doom Painting in St Thomas's Church ...* MA thesis, Open University

11   Benson, R and Hatcher, H, 1843, *Old and New Sarum, or Salisbury*, 589-90 and plate. Miss Wickens, a descendant of Sir Isaac Newton, lived in the Close, and was still alive in 1865, when she exhibited this and other drawings: *WANHM* vol 10 (1866), 34

12   *WANHM*, 1909, vol 36 ,18-19 and plate opp 185

13   Duke, E, 1837, *Prolusiones historicae, or the Halle of John Halle*, 545

14   Ashby, 180

15   *VCH Glos* vol 10 (1972) 28 and plate opp 33

16   Ashby, 344

17   Gill, M, c2005, The meaning of the doom, in Holy Trinity Church Coventry, *The Last Judgement: the Coventry Doom Painting and Holy Trinity Church*, 6-17

18   Examples below from Ashby, 266, 320, 335, 352

19   Owst, G R, 1961, *Literature and pulpit in medieval England*, 2nd ed, 243-84

20   Examples below from Timmins, T C B, 1984, *The Register of John Chandler, dean of Salisbury 1404-17* (Wilts Record Soc 39), xviii-xxi

21   Rosewell, 128, 296

22   Ashby, 179-81

23   Ibid, 168

24   Edwards .This identification has been challenged by Miriam Gill, who interprets it as a portrayal of the Seven Deadly Sins and Seven Corporal Works of Mercy: see www.le.ac.uk/ha/seedcorn/contents.html (accessed 29 April 2012). See also Rosewell, 86. I am most grateful to Ellie Pridgeon and Roger Rosewell for this reference.

25   H Shortt, H, revised Chandler, J, 2007, *The Giant and Hobnob*, 4th ed, 2

26   Edwards, 198; but see the alternative interpretation by Miriam Gill, above note 24

27   Salisbury Cathedral Archives, Chapter Act Book, Burgh, p1, *recto* and *verso*; see Haskins 133-6

28   Tatton Brown esp 104-7

29   Translated in Haskins, 292

30   For Moleyns and Upton, see *Oxford DNB*

31   Chandler, J, 2010, The feast of the not so innocents: a Christmas story, *Regional Historian* (UWE Bristol) no 22, 10-13

32   Hare, J, 1982, The Wiltshire risings of 1450: political and economic discontent in mid-fifteenth century England, *Southern History* vol 4, 13-31

33   Street, 227

34   Hollaender, 362-3

35   Sisam, K, 1921, *Fourteenth century verse and prose*, 125. I am grateful to Keith Blake for discussing this point and supplying the reference

36   Brown, A D, 1995, *Popular piety in late medieval England: diocese of Salisbury 1250-1550*, Oxford University Press, 202-22

37   The controversies described in this and the next paragraph are detailed in Street 227-57, and Haskins, 147-59

38   Street, 239, n2

39   Tatton Brown, 107

40   RCHM, 1993, *Salisbury: the Houses of the Close*, 45, 54. I am grateful to Tim Tatton Brown for pointing out the portcullis

41   *Oxford DNB* (sv Halle and Beauchamp)

42   *Ibid* (sv Woodville)

Old Sarum,
the Pitts and their Diamond.
The Origins of a Political Dynasty

David Richards

On the edge of Salisbury in the former village of Stratford sub Castle there sits an exquisite old house of mellow stone known as Mawarden Court. On its roadside garden wall a blue plaque indicates that William Pitt the Elder had spent part of his childhood there with the owner of the house, his grandfather, Thomas Pitt (1653-1722).

1940s watercolour of Mawarden Court by J Merritt. Copyright Victoria & Albert Museum.

Across the road an inscription carved on the tower of St Laurence's church states 'Tho. Pitt Esq.Benefactor. Erected 1711'. At the eastern side of the village, not far from the site of the Parliament Tree[1], on a great sarsen stone, another plaque commemorates the years that William Pitt the Elder (1708-78) served as MP for Old Sarum. Dominating the whole of the village is the dark bulk of the ancient fortress of Old Sarum, a rotten borough that had been the gateway to political power for many members of the Pitt family. The proximity of the plaques, the church inscription and a parliamentary seat on the edge of Salisbury hints at the complexity of their relationship.

A continent away from Salisbury in India, the old Fort St George in Madras survives as the site where Thomas Pitt made the fortune that enabled him to buy Old Sarum. He became governor of Fort St George and exerted a significant influence in the strengthening of England's foothold on the Coromandel Coast.

Nearer to home, in Paris, the Louvre Museum still jealously guards one of the world's most valuable gems, the Regent Diamond that was sold to the French state by Salisbury resident Thomas Pitt. The purpose of this paper is to examine these associations by looking at the life of Thomas Pitt (1653-1722)[2] as a merchant, English politician and Indian governor and will also include notes on his immediate family, his descendants and the role of his great diamond. It will include a brief account of the Pitt family's ownership of Old Sarum from its purchase in 1689 to its sale by another Thomas Pitt (1775-1804) in 1802.

Early Days

Thomas Pitt was born on 5 July 1653, the second son of the rector of Blandford St Mary in Dorset. The Rev John Pitt and his wife Sarah had nine children, of whom five survived, to be brought up on his relatively small stipend of £100 per annum.[3] When his father died in 1672, Thomas Pitt realised that he was going to have to make his own way in the world with virtually no help from his family. Nothing is known of his education or early life until he signed on as mate on board the *Lancaster*, an East Indiaman, in 1673 when he was a penniless 19 year old. It may be assumed he had possibly gained some earlier experience as a sailor out of the busy port of Poole, not far from Blandford. As soon as the *Lancaster* reached Balasore on the Bay of Bengal, Pitt jumped ship and peremptorily left the employ of the East India Company[4]. The East India Company had been set up under a charter of Queen Elizabeth I and continued under one granted by Charles II in 1661 giving the Company the right to trade in the East to the exclusion of all other subjects of the English king. However its employees were paid low wages so that many traded independently for their own benefit. Pitt joined their number and was labelled as an interloper for trading in defiance of the East India Company's monopoly and threatened with arrest. However, he was fortunate in obtaining help from Matthias Vincent of Hughli, the chief officer of the Company in Bengal, and Richard Edwards, chief of the factory at Balasore. Pitt embarked on many arduous years of work for Vincent during which he traded in horses from Persia and Indian sugar and chintzes whilst all the time learning about the customs and traditions of the locals and the best areas in which to operate as a merchant. Eventually, he amassed enough capital to trade exclusively on his own behalf. In 1679 he married Jane Innes[5], the niece of Matthias Vincent. In 1681 Thomas, Jane and their baby son Robert returned to England on an interloper's ship, the *William and John,* with a valuable cargo of their own goods.

The Council of the East India Company were frustrated and angered to hear that the interloper Pitt had arrived in England with such wealth. They decided to punish him in the courts but he was too quick for them and rapidly left for India on board another interloping ship. The East India Company immediately sent instructions for his arrest, but failed to detain him. After this further successful trading session Pitt returned again to England in1683 on the *Crown* in possession of an extremely lucrative assortment of merchandise. At this juncture Pitt was arrested and imprisoned for a week before being fined £1000 for interloping. In the event he only paid £400 of the fine.

Initial successes

Comfortably established as a wealthy gentleman, Pitt was able to purchase, in 1688, Mawarden Court and in the elections of 1689 became MP for Old Sarum. He was following in the footsteps of many opportunist politicians who had used it to gain entry to Parliament and its lucrative sphere of influence in Westminster. His outright purchase of Old Sarum in 1691 eventually enabled him, his sons and his famous grandson William Pitt the Elder all to obtain seats in Parliament. Unfortunately for Pitt the 1689 election was contested by Thomas Mompesson and parliament declared the election to be void on 16 March 1689.[6] Fortunately for Pitt he was soon elected as MP for Salisbury. He represented Salisbury continuously for six years from 1689-95, even retaining the seat during a further stay in India from 1693. The question arises as to why after ten years of a comfortable life as a London politician and a country landowner he decided to leave in 1693 and embark on such a difficult activity as an independent trader in Bengal. Years later, his great grandson, Lord Camelford, noted that Pitt was then in a syndicate of merchants who financed the galley *Arcana as* a privateer, to prey on French shipping in the English Channel. He was captured after joining the privateers on board the *Arcana* (he was, after all, a competent sailor who had liked to be addressed as captain). This resulted in such a financial disaster for Pitt that he needed another Indian trading season to recoup his losses.[7]

Governor of Madras

When Pitt arrived in India in 1693 a long running dispute between those who controlled the old East India Company and those who wanted a new company was

The Pitt Diamond

This remarkable Indian diamond helped to fund an English political dynasty with a Salisbury base, became part of the French crown jewels, and survived the revolution to adorn kings and emperors before being consigned in modern times to a vault.

Having survived the hazardous journey from India in 1702 it took another two years in London to complete the technically difficult task of cutting such a valuable stone. Pitt sold the off cuts to Peter the Great for £7000, but despite a meeting with King George II and the Prince of Wales he was unable to sell the gem to the English crown. Pitt displays it on his hat in the Vanderbank portrait of himself as a gentleman.

Finally his persistence paid off and he struck a deal with the Regent of France selling the stone for £125,000. The diamond, now known as the Regent, entered the French crown jewels and was placed in Louis XV's and Louis XVI's crown. Later Marie Antoinette wore it in her hat. At the height of the French Revolution all the crown jewels were stolen in Paris but the diamond was later recovered. Napoleon used it on the hilt of his sword. Following changes in the ruling regime, the diamond was mounted successively on the crowns of Louis XVIII, Charles X and Napoleon III, and finally on the Grecian diadem of Empress Eugénie. In 1887 it was placed in the Louvre Museum where it remains to this day, although it has been withdrawn from public display due to its great value. However it is possible to see in the British Museum the rock crystal copy commissioned by Pitt, who was ever fearful of robbery, to enable him to safely show it to potential buyers.

unresolved, although the courts had decided that it was legal for Englishmen to trade independently in the East. Two years later, in 1695, Pitt returned to England with a fortune greater than that he had ever made before. Eventually the old Company decided unanimously, in November 1697, that the extensive Indian knowledge and the confident, masterful character of Thomas Pitt, their former enemy, could be used to their advantage and they appointed him as President of the Coromandel Coast and Governor of Fort St George in Madras.

During his voyage to India the monopoly of the Eastern trade was passed by Parliament to a new company with the proviso that the Old Company's rights should be retained for three years.[8] In September 1698 he arrived at Fort St George with his 18 year old son Robert. Twelve months later the new company's officials arrived in India and a bitter struggle ensued between them. The new company men so upset the Mogul emperor Aurangezeb that his general Daud Khan besieged the English in Madras. Pitt resisted with great skill and eventually triumphantly negotiated the withdrawal of the attackers[9] and greatly enhanced the reputation of the English in India, enabling the Old Company to obtain favourable concessions from Aurangezeb. After three years the two companies amalgamated and Pitt stayed on as Governor until 1709.

England and the Diamond

In 1698, at his appointment as Governor, Pitt had left his pregnant wife Jane and two sons (Thomas and William) and two daughters (Essex and Lucy) living in considerable comfort in Mawarden Court. A few months later another son, John was born. A year later Pitt writes to his wife at Old Sarum 'I hope you look after my plantations, Gardens &ca. as I Desir, that I may find 'em on my returne in a good Condition. My blessing to the Children, of whose education pray takes great Care.'[10] Pitt had left the conduct of his business affairs in England solely in the hands of his wife (although she was advised by two of Pitt's East India Company friends). Pitt would send goods back to England relying on his agent and his wife Jane to sell them and return money and bullion[11] for him to continue his activities as a merchant.

Jane was an intermittent letter writer and even worse at sending money and silver

The mansion of Boconnoc in Cornwall, set in a 5,000 area estate. This was one of a number of properties purchased by Thomas Pitt that illustrated his considerable wealth. The picture taken by D.Richards,in 2010, with the kind permission of Mr & Mrs A.Fortescue.'

from Salisbury to her husband. Pitt's enemies spread scurrilous rumours about Jane and when news of her visits to Bath (with suggestions of fast living and visits to the gaming tables) reached Pitt he decided to make a permanent break with his wife.[12]

He had another problem to trouble him. This had stemmed from a visit during the siege of Fort St George by an Indian trader offering for sale a fabulously large and flawless diamond. It was over 400 carats. Pitt could not resist and after protracted negotiations he knocked down the price from £100,000 to £25,000 and bought it. He then entrusted to his son Robert to take it to England hidden in the hollow heel of his shoe. Unfortunately for Pitt, his son Robert led an even more profligate life and communicated even less frequently with his father than his mother had done. Robert also married without seeking his father's permission and spent £500 (Pitt said it could be done for £10) getting himself elected MP for Old Sarum. Pitt became wildly enraged with his family's ingratitude and their lack of concern for him. He once described in a letter 'the hellish confusion that is my family'.[13] In his absence the great diamond was cut and the fragments sold to Peter the Great for £7000. News of the fate of the diamond was excruciatingly slow in arriving in Madras causing Pitt great anxiety. In total he spent 15 years trying to get heads of state to buy his diamond before finally managing to sell it to the Regent of France in 1717.[14]

Success

When Pitt arrived back home in 1710 he was famous, respected and considered to be extraordinarily rich. He set about acquiring property. His possessions ultimately included Boconnoc, a 5000 acre estate in Cornwall, a large London townhouse in Pall Mall, Swallowfield, a mansion set on an estate near Reading, the manor of Abbot's Ann in Hampshire and the Rectory and Manor of his birthplace Blandford St Mary. He restored St Lawrence's Church in Stratford sub Castle, re-building its tower as well as paying for new silverware and the superbly carved royal arms. He also restored his father's old church at Blandford St Mary. His purchase of the Mohun estates in Devon gave Governor Pitt access to another rotten borough at Okehampton, which the family used when Old Sarum was unavailable. In 1715 he was a commissioner for building 50 new churches in and around London and was appointed as Governor of Jamaica in 1716-1717 but never took up the post.

Vanderbank's sumptuous and high status portrait[15] of a vigorous, autocratic Governor Pitt prominently displays alongside him on a tricorn hat the source of his wealth and reputation, his eponymous diamond. It is a rare image showing a man and his possession combining to project a supremely confident statement of power to contemporary society. With this aura of influence and great wealth Pitt was able to move in a circle that contained important merchants, politicians and aristocratic landowners. His five Salisbury children generally married well (his sixth, William, had died of smallpox as a child). Lucy married General James Stanhope (later Earl Stanhope) in 1712. She was to spend her last days at her home at Chevening, which is now the Foreign Secretary's official residence.

Essex married Charles Cholmondley in 1714. John was married to Lady Mary Belasyse, the daughter of Viscount Fauconberg. Thomas married Lady Francis Ridgeway, daughter of the Earl of Londonderry, a title that Thomas would inherit. He later became the Governor of the Leeward Islands. Robert, the eldest, had married Harriet Villiers whose grandson, another Thomas Pitt, became the first Earl of Camelford.

Old Sarum MPs

Year	MPs
1689	Thomas Pitt[16]
1695	William Harvey I Thomas Pitt
1698	William Harvey I Charles Mompesson
1701	William Harvey I Charles Mompesson
1701	William Harvey I Charles Mompesson
1702	William Harvey I Charles Mompesson
1705	Robert Pitt Charles Mompesson John Fitzgerald Villiers, Viscount Grandison double return of Mompesson and Viscount Grandison. Mompesson declared elected, 11 Dec 1705 Robert Pitt
1708	William Harvey I Robert Pitt
1710	Thomas Pitt William Harvey II
1713	Thomas Pitt Robert Pitt
1715	Thomas Pitt senior Robert Pitt Richard Jones Charles Tucker
1716	Sir William Strickland *vice* Thomas Pitt, appointed to office
1720	Strickland re-elected after appointment to office
1722	Thomas Pitt sen. Robert Pitt
1722	George Morton Pitt *vice* Robert Pitt chose to sit for Okehampton
1724	John Pitt *vice* George Morton Pitt, appointed to office
1726	George Pitt *vice* Thomas Pitt senior deceased
1727	Thomas Pitt junior Thomas Pitt, Earl of Londonderry
1728	Matthew Chitty St Quintin, *vice* Thomas Pitt, chose to sit for Okehampton
1728	Thomas Harrison *vice* Londonderry, appointed to office
1734	Thomas Pitt Robert Nedham
1735	William Pitt *vice* Thomas Pitt chose to sit for Okehampton
1741	William Pitt George Lyttelton
1742	James Grenville *vice* Lyttelton chose to sit for Okehampton
1746	Grenville re-elected after appointment to office 26 Feb 1746 Pitt re-elected after appointment to office

1746	Pitt re-elected after appointment to office
1747	Edward Willes vice Grenville, appointed to office
1747	Thomas Pitt Sir William Irby
1801	John Horne Tooke *vice* Yonge, vacated his seat

In terms of sheer numbers, the Pitt family in Parliament reached a peak in the 1720s when Governor Pitt was MP for Thirsk, his son Robert was MP for Old Sarum, his son Thomas was MP for Wilton and his youngest son John was MP for Hindon. To have

Old Sarum

Old Sarum is a unique and powerful structure with a story that spans the millennia. It was created as a massive hill fort some 2500 years ago by an Iron Age tribal society to dominate the surrounding landscape. Recognised by subsequent invaders for its strategic importance near the confluence of five valleys, it has witnessed many changes. The Romans marched their legions to it. The Saxons used the fort as a safe haven from Viking predation. When the Normans came they extended the fortifications by digging another vast circular ditch and mound inside the hill fort to protect a new castle keep and a royal residence. In 1075 the building of a cathedral was started in the outer bailey, adding the pervasive power of the church to that of the king in the castle. But this was to sow the seeds of division that ultimately led to the hill's abandonment and the establishment of the city of New Sarum in the valley below. From the 14th century the owners of a largely de-populated Old Sarum were able to send two Members of Parliament to London. This privilege could (and did) change hands for money. For over four hundred years this inequitable and corrupt practice gave Old Sarum the reputation as one of the country's worst rotten boroughs. Thomas Pitt saw the long term advantages to himself and his family and eventually gained ownership of what Cobbett was to describe as the 'accursed hill'. The Reform Act of 1832 swept away Old Sarum's political power leaving the crumbling fortress gradually to take on its new role as an attraction for visitors intent on exploring its colourful history. The entrepreneurial 'Diamond' Pitt would surely have approved that a charge is made today for entry to the castle.

Inscription on the tower of St Lawrence Church in Stratford sub Castle, dated 1711.

four members of the same family sitting in the same Parliament was an extraordinary achievement.

Governor Pitt's first son Robert sat in seven Parliaments continuously, from 1705 to his death in 1727, four times for Old Sarum, once for Salisbury (1710-1713), and twice for Okehampton. He represented Old Sarum from 1705-1710 and from 1713-1722. In 1710 he gave £500 to Salisbury Workhouse.[17] After inheriting the bulk of his father's estate he survived for only a year to die of the stone in 1727.

Governor Pitt's second son Thomas represented Wilton from 1713-1727 and was its mayor 1711-17. He was MP for Old Sarum from 1727-February 1728. He is said to have lost over £50,000 in the South Sea Bubble. The third son John also represented Old Sarum from 1724 to 1727. His father described him as a 'good for nothing Colonel'.[18] He fell out with his father and being short of money waited outside the Governor's Pall Mall house for the agent to arrive with the estate rents and then entered with his sword drawn, scooped up the money and ran off. Cut off from his father's will he died in relative poverty in Hammersmith.

Governor Pitt's grandson William Pitt the Elder was MP for Old Sarum from 1735 to 1746. His abilities and achievements were recognised by all and encapsulated by Churchill who wrote that the spirit of Pitt was to 'make the Union Jack supreme in every ocean, to conquer, to command, and never to count the cost, whether in blood or

THIS STONE
ERECTED BY THE CORPORATION OF NEW SARUM
COMMEMORATES THAT NEAR THIS SPOT
BENEATH THE SPREADING BRANCHES OF AN ELM TREE
MEMBERS OF PARLIAMENT FOR THE BOROUGH OF OLD SARUM
WERE IN FORMER TIMES ELECTED MOST NOTABLE OF WHOM WAS

WILLIAM PITT

AFTERWARDS EARL OF CHATHAM
"CLARUM ET VENERABILE NOMEN GENTIBUS
ET MULTUM NOSTRAE QUOD PRODERAT URBI"
WHO FORGED THOSE LINKS OF EMPIRE WHICH NOW
BIND OUR FELLOW CITIZENS BEYOND THE SEAS
IN AFFECTION TO THE MOTHER COUNTRY.

WHEREFORE LET THIS PLACE BE FOR EVER ENSHRINED
IN THE HEARTS OF OUR COUNTRYMEN.

THIS SITE WAS RESTORED, AND A NEW ELM TREE PLANTED,
BY SALISBURY M.P. ROBERT KEY, ON 7TH JUNE 2000 FOLLOWING
COLLABORATION BETWEEN ENGLISH HERITAGE, ORDNANCE SURVEY,
SALISBURY DISTRICT COUNCIL AND WILTSHIRE WILDLIFE TRUST.

Memorial plaque to William Pitt the Elder on the Portway leading from Old Sarum.

gold'. It is interesting that he presented a Reform Bill in 1747 that would have eliminated the Rotten Borough of Old Sarum. The bill was defeated.

The Loss of Old Sarum

Thomas Pitt, second Baron Camelford (1775-1804),[19] was the last member of the Pitt family to own Old Sarum. He was a naval officer and a notorious rake. In 1791 he joined, as a midshipman, HMS *Discovery*, commanded by Capt George Vancouver on an exploratory voyage into the Pacific. He was flogged several times for insubordination, placed in irons and discharged in Hawaii. On returning to London still smouldering from this humiliation he met Vancouver in Conduit Street and publicly thrashed him with his cane. Later serving as a Lieutenant in the West Indies he shot and killed a fellow officer in an alleged mutiny. The court martial acquitted him. In 1801 he backed the Rev John Horne Tooke as MP for Old Sarum. Parliament was not in favour of this action and later introduced a law banning priests from serving as MPs.

Pitt was so incensed that the following year he sold Old Sarum for £40,000 to Du Pré Alexander, 2nd Earl of Caledon. Pitt was killed, aged 29, by a pistol shot in a duel fought over a woman.[20]

Conclusions

During the hundred years or so that the Pitts owned Old Sarum it is possible to trace character traits in the family that may have originated in Governor Pitt. Few of his descendants appear to have inherited his bold even courageous approach to entrepreneurial trading but many of them demonstrated a tendency towards a volcanic, irascible temper.[21] Some of them were plagued with melancholia and depression; both Pitt the Elder and Pitt the Younger suffered from days of dense blackness. But they all, from the Governor onwards, enjoyed their drink. Pitt the Younger regularly drank a bottle of port a day.

The life of Thomas Pitt demonstrates how a penniless young man in the late 1600s (if he had a driving ambition and a steely determination) could acquire a great fortune from trading in the East. His wealth enabled him to enter parliament by means of the rotten borough of Old Sarum and move in the highest social circles, mingling with successful merchants, politicians and aristocrats. The firm financial and political base created by him proved to be a great advantage to his family who all married well. It is arguable that without his money and his ownership of Old Sarum, the William Pitts, Elder and Younger, may never have been able to rise to their dizzy heights.

It may also be argued that the Pitt family's political success only served to emphasise the gross inequality of English governance in general and rotten boroughs in particular. During the debates that led to the reform movement in the 1830s Old Sarum was cited as a classic example of electoral corruption.

David Richards is a retired dental surgeon who is now a Blue Badge guide with a particular interest in the history of the people and the buildings of the Salisbury area.

Bibliography and Notes

Barlow, R and Yule, H (eds), 1889, *The diary of William Hedges … during his agency in Bengal; as well as on his voyage out and return overland (1681–1687)*, Vol 3, Hakluyt Society, 78
Dalton, Sir Cornelius Neale, 1915, *The Life of Thomas Pitt*, Cambridge University Press
Lever, Sir Tresham, 1947, *The House of Pitt*, John Murray
Oxford Dictionary of National Biography 2012, online edition, accessed 2012
Rosebery, Lord, 1910, *Lord Chatham, his early life and connections*, Harper.
The History of Parliament: www.historyofparliamentonline.org, accessed 2012
Tolstoy, Nikolai, 1978, *The Half Mad Lord, Thomas Pitt 2nd Baron Camelford*, Jonathan Cape.

Notes

1 The History of Parliament: www.historyofparliamentonline.org, accessed March 2012. Elections were held under the 'parliamentary tree' in the 'electing acre', the field 'where the last houses are supposed to have stood'

2 DNB Online edition accessed March 2012

3 Dalton,7

4 Dalton, 9

5 Lever, 4

6 History of Parliament website, *Old Sarum*

7 Dalton, 74-5

8 Dalton, 143-163 The New East India Company was created under a charter granted by William III in 1698.

9 Diary of William Hedges, 85

10 Diary of William Hedges. In a letter dated Dec 4, 1701 from a Mr John Philips, a neighbour, who writes from Stratford with news of Pitt's plantations and the suggestion that the inner circle of the castle might be levelled to plant more trees. There is also a brief account of the November election at Old Sarum with a complaint about a voter.

11 The European price of bullion, mainly silver and pieces of eight was less than the Indian. Uncut Indian diamonds were attractively priced so English merchants were able to trade bullion for goods and diamonds at very advantageous rates.

12 Dalton, 386-404

13 Rosebery, 8

14 Dalton, 520

15 Today it hangs in Chevening House, Kent, once the home of Pitt's daughter Lucy and her husband Earl Stanhope. It was painted by John Vanderbank (1694-1739) who was a pupil of Kneller.

16 This list of Old Sarum MPs is from The History of Parliament: www.historyofparliamentonline.org, 2012

17 *Victoria County History of Wiltshire*, 1962, vol 6, p113.

18 Rosebery, 12, and Lever, 54

19 DNB Online accessed March 2012. The last member of the Pitt family to own Old Sarum is buried in St Anne's Church, Dean Street, Soho, London, an area in which Governor Pitt had purchased much property.

20 Tolstoy, 180

21 Rosebery, 7 'Thomas Pitt's blood came all aflame from the East and flowed like burning lava to his remotest descendants'.

1912 Salisbury 'Scout' Motor Car – AA 4476

Adrian Green

In 1902 William and Albert Burden, city clock makers since 1881, and Percy Dean, Chitterne landowner, who provided the initial capital, founded Dean and Burden Brothers, motor engineers. They had premises in Friary Lane, called the Excelsior works, where production began on marine boat engines. The following year they started

The Scout motor car today with the director of Salisbury and South Wiltshire Museum (copyright Caroline Rippier)

Albert and William Burden who established Scout Motors Limited in 1902

making 2½ and 3½ horsepower motor cycles, and in 1905, after the firm changed its name to Scout, their first cars were produced. The second one, driven by J P Dean, was entered for the Isle of Man Tourist Trophy Race, but unfortunately ran out of petrol before the end of the race. Entries were also made in the following two years, but again without success.[1] Each car took between six to eight weeks to make to personal specification and in the Salisbury district several of the early models were bought by doctors.

Initial success meant a move to larger premises at Churchfields, Bemerton, (on the site of the present firm 'Sydenhams'). Four standard models of cars were produced, and in 1909, motor delivery vans, an early model being bought by grocer Robert Stokes. With showrooms in Queen Street, the firm reached its peak in 1912 when two 'silent, speedy, superior vehicles', capable of average speeds of 40-50mph were produced each week and 150 men employed.[2] Cars cost from between £265 and £730, all parts were made on site, down to the nuts and bolts and the firm was the largest employer in the city. Scout buses were produced to replace the horse drawn carriers and ran successfully for many years helping to revolutionise the carrying trade.

When the First World War started in 1914 the firm continued production but the vehicles were mainly for military and governmental purposes. The next year new machinery was installed for munitions work, to make bombs and mechanisms for magnetic mines. In 1920 the firm was relieved of all war contacts and peacetime production resumed. This included 3 and 4 ton lorries,15.9 hp pleasure cars and Pullmans and charabancs. However the firm never recovered its pre-war prosperity and the expensive Scout cars simply could not compete with cheap mass-produced cars of Ford and Morris and in 1921 the company was wound up and went into voluntary liquidation.

AA 4476 was manufactured at the Scout Works, Lower Road, Bemerton, Salisbury and first registered at Winchester in 1912. Little is known of its early history. On 6 February 1925 the logbook shows the owner to be Mr Chas Radford, Sunnyside Garage, Sampford Peverell, Devon. Three days later the car was transferred to Mr Edgar Jarvis in Sampford Peverell whose name remained on the log book until 1950 when the Timmis Brothers of Yeovil rescued the Scout from a scrap yard in Honiton. Fortunately it was virtually complete and almost entirely original. All the original brasswork survives

Photo of 4-Cylinder 12/14 H.P. "Scout" Car, Torpedo Body.   15.9.

Standard Price   =   £340

With extras as shown, viz.: Hood Screen, Spare Steel Wheel with Tyre on same, and two Head Lights.

£380

A similar model advertised in the 1912 Scout Motors catalogue

AA4476 under restoration

including the tail lamp, side lamps, head lamps and acetylene generator. In 1952 Mr George Bond of Yeovil bought the car in the as-found condition. He carried out a partial restoration, including reupholstering in 'Rexine' (a modern synthetic material) and repainting the car in 'chamois', a rather dull brown colour. It was rallied during the period 1952 to 1956 (including the Coronation Rally in June 1953). Some time later it was blocked up in a garage until purchased by the present Salisbury based owners in 1984.

From 1984 to 1990 the car underwent a complete restoration, preceded by extensive research. It was stripped down to every last nut and bolt and all parts were cleaned down to bare metal before reassembly. Replacement wheels were provided by Beaulieu Motor Museum. The logbook shows that the colour was dark green in the 1920s. Traces of original green paint were found during stripping down so the body has been painted in Brunswick green with primrose yellow coach lining. The chassis has been hand-painted in black and the seats reupholstered in black button-back leather. The original hood sticks have been re-covered in an authentic black canvas material.

In the 1990s the car was rallied on several occasions. In 1991 at the Breamore VCC Classic Car Show it won the Veteran/Edwardian Concours award and in 1995 the

Allday Best Restored trophy awarded by the Veteran Car Club of Great Britain, South West Section.

It is only one of two Scout Cars believed to be extant. It is not only the older but because of the detailed care taken during restoration it is also a truly representative example of a Scout Motor Car produced at the time. The car should be seen as a true example of Salisbury's industrial heritage of which the city can be proud. Salisbury Museum has been offered the opportunity to buy the Scout Car from the present owners. The Museum believes the Scout should stay in Salisbury for future generations to enjoy. It would also make a striking centre piece in a new museum gallery dedicated to Salisbury's recent past. As *Sarum Chronicle* goes to press the Museum has raised over £25,000 towards the £40,000 purchase price – including grants of £5,000 from Salisbury City Council and £5,000 from Wiltshire Council.

For more details or offers of support please contact Museum Director Adrian Green at Salisbury Museum on 01722 332151 or email: museum@salisburymuseum.or.uk

Adrian Green has a degree in archaeology from University College London, a master's in museum studies from Leicester University, and is an associate member of the Museums Association. He became director of Salisbury Museum in 2007. He lives in Salisbury with his wife and three children.

Notes

1 www.gracesguides.co.uk, for 1905, 1906 and 1907 Tourist Trophy Races, accessed June 2012. *The Times* 1906, Aug 29, p9; Sep 26, p9; Sep 29, p9;1907 31 May, p12; 1 June, p16.

2 Farrant, J, 1967, *Scout Motors Limited of Salisbury*, Salisbury and South Wiltshire Group for Industrial Archaeology

Further Reading

Daniels, P, 1992, *Salisbury in Old Photographs, a third selection*, Alan Sutton.Section one is devoted to Scout Motors and contains numerous pictures of Scout vehicles.

Hicks, I, 2006, ed, *Early Motor Vehicle Registration in Wiltshire 1903-1914*, Wiltshire Record Society, 58. This shows that 147 cars were registered in Wiltshire between 1903-1914 (xiv).

A Prospering Society

Wiltshire in the later Middle Ages

Studies in Regional and Local History
Volume 10

John Hare

Book Reviews

A Prospering Society: Wiltshire in the later middle ages, by John Hare, (University of Hertfordshire Press), *Studies in Regional and Local History* 10, 2011, xvi, 240pp, hardback,
£35.00, ISBN 978-1-902806-84-6
(also paperback, 2012, £18.99, ISBN 978-1-902806-85-3).

John Hare completed his doctoral thesis on Wiltshire's late medieval landlords and their tenants in 1976 and, until his recent retirement, has pursued a distinguished teaching career in Winchester. The intervening 35 years have seen a stream of scholarly papers from his pen (20 are cited in the bibliography), largely concerned with medieval society in Wiltshire and Hampshire. This book, therefore, is the long-awaited distillation of an unrivalled store of research and wisdom. Moreover it is the first full-length study of Wiltshire's medieval economic history since the multi-faceted *Victoria History* volume 4 half a century ago, and – I think – the first ever treatment of this crucial period of the county's history by a single author.

So we should expect an important and stimulating book, which is exactly what we are given. The author divides his treatment into three parts. The first places Wiltshire in its national context, describes the county and its tenurial structure, and discusses the difficulties of using the available sources – which are principally the manorial records of major institutional landlords. He focuses on the period 1380–1520, with a substantial glance back to agriculture before and in the immediate aftermath of the Black Death.

The book's second part, occupying nearly half the text, tackles the rural scene. Although the treatment aims to be countywide, the sources are more prolific for chalkland manors, especially those owned by the Winchester institutions of bishop, cathedral and college. Downton and Durrington furnish evidence for agricultural practice and peasant mobility, and the predictable themes of sheep-corn regimes and demesne leasing are explored in great detail. Dr Hare's work on the latter, in this book and elsewhere, has made him a respected authority, and must surely be essential reading far beyond Wiltshire. Sheep were important, of course, and their numbers and importance grew during the 15th century, but other livestock claim the historian's attention too, notably pigs, and some downland farmers tried commercial rabbit farming on a large scale – diversification is nothing new.

It is in the book's final section, devoted to industry and commerce, that the Salisbury historian will find most to chew over. Dr Hare has described elsewhere in some detail the city's career during the 15th century,[1] but here he is able to set it in the context of the county and region of which it was the capital. In three chapters the book considers the role that towns played in stimulating and controlling trade; and the hugely important and dynamic cloth industry; and then offers a chronology, of growth, recession and recovery. Salisbury features heavily in all three.

Some of his conclusions about Salisbury come as no surprise – the city's pattern of overseas and domestic trade, for instance, in finished cloth, dyestuffs, wine and fish. But it is reassuring to find a historian from Hampshire agreeing that 'Southampton became a virtual outport of Salisbury' (p153, reiterated on p170). There is much new, or at least previously unconsidered material, on the importance of the leather trade, for example (pp165-6), and the number of foreigners (96 in 1440) who were living in the city (pp155-5). There are some startling statistics too. In 1394/5 Salisbury appears to have been responsible for nearly 90% of Wiltshire's cloth output; this had fallen to 70% in 1414/15, and under 23% in 1467 (p183). But this was not a symptom of a city in freefall industrial decline, rather an indication of the astonishing advance in clothmaking in west and north-west Wiltshire.

To most people, local historians included, medieval England may seem distant and static. Not least of the many accomplishments of this masterly book is Dr Hare's vivid portrayal of a restless society, an era of opportunity for innovative entrepreneurs, and a dynamic and fluctuating economy. This is a book which anyone embarking on a study of a Wiltshire town or village should consult, and it is particularly relevant for the student of Salisbury, the city on which so many of its themes converge.

John Chandler

Note

1   John Hare, 2009, 'Salisbury: the economy of a fifteenth-century provincial capital', *Southern History* 31, 1-26

Jane Howells and Ruth Newman, (eds), *William Small's*
Cherished Memories and Associations,
Wiltshire Record Society 64 (2011), pp. lxvii + 160, £20
ISBN 978-0-901333-41-4

William Small (1820-1890), a Salisbury painter and glazier, combined elements of memoirs, local chronicle, memorandum book, autobiography and diary in the two manuscript volumes presented in this excellent edition, with its helpful introduction, indexes, family trees and notes. It will henceforth be an indispensable source not only for the history of Salisbury itself, but also for studies of nineteenth-century business, religion, politics and family relations. Small's father, William Senior (1789?-1863), built up the family painting and glazing business. He served as a member of the Salisbury grand jury and in 1842-3 as an overseer of the poor for St Martin's parish. His widow carried on his business after his death. Our author, his eldest son, married Elizabeth Sutton, one of the daughters of a prosperous Salisbury baker, in 1852. Their son died in 1870, followed by Elizabeth in 1875. William seems to have written his two volumes in 1881. They occupied and diverted him at a time when he faced severe difficulties in finding enough work to pay his rent and his brother John's wages. Eventually he entered the Trinity Hospital, an almshouse for old men of Salisbury.

Small's principal declared aim in recording his memories was to write about his 'Dear & Honoured father and mother'. He regarded them and his younger sister Henrietta as his 'three best earthly friends'. When compiling his record in 1881 he still felt deeply the comparatively recent loss of his mother and Henrietta in 1877, and usually visited his family's burial place in Britford churchyard on Sundays, placing a nosegay on his sister's grave. By contrast he said next to nothing about his wife or son. The editors suggest, very plausibly, that the marriage was probably unhappy. Elizabeth gave birth to their only child before they were married. Perhaps the couple yielded to a transient passion that doomed them to a loveless union. William's record presents him as a man who looked back to childhood and young adulthood as his happiest times, and one whose affections were concentrated on his family of birth. His 'Cherished Memories' are suffused with nostalgia and a self-pity against which William fought with limited success by counting his blessings.

Much of William's record consists of vivid vignettes of the Smalls' patrons and customers, and descriptions of the glazing and painting work the family undertook for them. Particularly valuable for the business historian is evidence concerning the difficulties the Smalls encountered in securing prompt and full payment. Several customers objected to estimates or bills, or failed to settle until long after the original bill had been presented. The Smalls' best customers were gentry, lay or clerical. Henry Parr Hamilton, Dean of Salisbury from 1850 to 1880, was 'the greatest help we ever had'. Such patronage helped to ensure that the Smalls often voted Tory before the advent of the secret ballot despite their membership of the Methodist church in Salisbury. Some of William's father's fellow dissenters resented his failure to support the Liberal cause in two 1843 by-elections so much that they withheld their custom. The firm seems to have prospered nonetheless. By 1881, however, William's advancing years and melancholy may have proved increasing handicaps in the competition with more vigorous and adaptable business rivals.

Ralph Houlbrooke
Professor Emeritus in history at University of Reading
(This review was first published in *Southern History*)

Salisbury: The struggle for Reform. The 180th anniversary of the great Reform Act, 1832

Ruth Newman

'When the news arrived ... the joy of our townsmen knew no bounds. Salisbury
has never in our time known a happier day'.

Salisbury Journal: 21 May 1832

Not the ending of a war, nor the birth of a prince, not even a projected railway, but the news that the king, William IV, had recalled his prime minister, Earl Grey, and that the passing of the Reform Bill was now virtually certain.

This extraordinary jubilation hints at the passionate commitment from some citizens in the struggle for reform in the city. In 2012 it is difficult to conjure up the sense of involvement and real excitement that existed at the time. It was an issue which dominated both national and regional politics, and the local paper, the *Salisbury and Winchester Journal*, broadcast the intense political fervour for over 18 months between 1830 and 1832, culminating in the gaining of the vote by an important group of citizens.

This paper is not intended as a commentary on Old Sarum, an extreme example of a rotten or pocket borough, but on the campaign within the city itself. The *Journal* chose hardly to mention Old Sarum, which long before 1832 had become both a laughing stock and a tourist attraction. American visitors from the 1780s came to Stratford sub Castle to mock our political system, where an enterprising local family supplied the 'curious who visit there with punch, wine and tea'.[1] Thomas Macaulay, ironically representing the rotten borough of Calne, stated in 1831 that 'under the present system, Manchester, with 200,000 inhabitants, has no members, Old Sarum, with no inhabitants, has two members.'[2] The electoral procedure was a farce; estimates of the actual number of electors vary but ranged from two to seven, voting under the 'Parliament Tree' for their landlord's two nominees. Parliament, by 1831, was almost unanimous in agreement that Old Sarum was a condemned borough and its disfranchisement was inevitable.

The real battle for political reform lay within the city itself and it proved an epoch-making period, interweaving local and national history in an extraordinary way.

Background: the unreformed system before 1832

General elections were held every seven years and mostly concerned local issues. In the 18th century there were no great political and rival parties in the modern sense, but by the early 19th century the issue of reform was dividing the parties. The Whigs supported reform and portrayed themselves as the friends of liberty who had embraced the causes of the Nonconformists and eventually the Roman Catholics. The Tories were reluctant to grant further political rights and clung to their image of defenders of the established church, the crown, and law and order.

There were elections for both counties and boroughs. Forty-one counties, whatever their size, each sent two MPs to Westminster. Voters had to possess a freehold worth 40 shillings (the '40s freeholder'), mainly landowners and prosperous businessmen.

All voting was *open* (until 1872) which could mean enormous bribery and expense. Electors simply mounted the steps of the hustings and publicly declared for their candidate. In the 1818 Wiltshire elections, the poll remained open for nine days; John Benett's supporters were dined every day at the White Hart in Salisbury whilst another candidate gave sumptuous dinners at Marlborough with singers and entertainment.

Voting in the boroughs was a lottery; 200 constituencies returned two MPs each and qualification varied from place to place. As a rough guide, no females and few poor had the vote, but a sizeable section of the middle classes was also excluded including those in Salisbury.

There were five main types of borough, and voting rights often depended upon some ancient formula going back centuries eg *pot-wallopers* or *scot and lot*.[3] In Salisbury only the *corporation* could vote while the *rotten borough* of Old Sarum was an obvious affront to democracy. In the early 19th century parliament was still composed mainly of landowners, often concerned with local issues such as enclosures, turnpike trusts and canals. The old agricultural interests of the rural south were over represented (Wiltshire had 34 MPs) while the new industrial cities of Birmingham, Manchester, Leeds and Sheffield had not a single member between them. By 1831 the population of the UK had grown to 24 million, the electorate was a mere 400,000 and parliament was increasingly out of touch with the people.

In 1830 the issue of parliamentary reform was brought out into the open. The new king, William IV, was more receptive to change and in November of that year Earl Grey formed a Whig government committed to reform.

Reform Act 1832

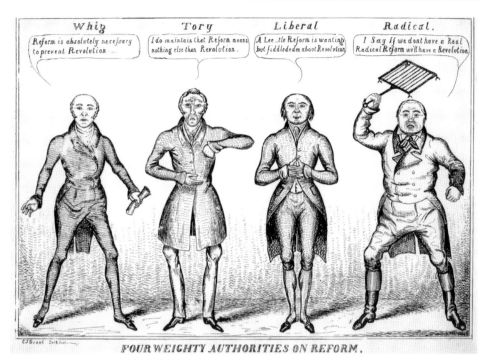

'Four Weighty Authorities on Reform' © British Library Board, (ADD 5247, folio 47)

Salisbury's population in 1831 was 9876[4] and the estimated number qualified to vote was 55 councillors. The MPs were the Tory, Wadham Wyndham who was strongly opposed to reform, and the aristocratic Whig, the Honourable Duncombe Pleydell Bouverie, who like his older brother, the 3rd Earl of Radnor in the House of Lords, supported the new government's measures. Indeed, the radical Lord Radnor of Longford Castle, a friend of William Cobbett, was one of the few local landlords to support reform. Wyndham and Bouverie had been returned unopposed by members of the council in the elections of July/August 1830. Despite the council claim to be 'honourably independent', a few years earlier a citizen had complained that the position was a *'farce'* because 'this city has not any voice in the senate, as one member's vote neutralises the other'.[5]

The *Salisbury Journal* played an interesting role; it reported all the events of the crisis in enormous detail. The local paper might not of course reflect contemporary views and in the absence of opinion polls we cannot know for certain how the people of Salisbury as a whole felt about this issue. The newspaper was crammed with the minutiae of parliamentary debates as well as the smallest local meeting, but the owner and editor was William Bird Brodie who increasingly became passionately involved in the reform movement. The more conservative *Devizes Gazette* and *Hampshire Advertiser* took a far more cautious and critical line. The *Journal's* reporting was certainly not impartial; Henry Hatcher struck a warning note when he commented that the question aroused more interest than any previous measure of national policy, but 'in this city a large and respectable portion of the inhabitants were opposed to the change, and the progress of the Bill was watched with extreme solicitude'.[6] Nevertheless the sense of involvement and later jubilation appears widespread.

The progress of the Reform Bill

The first Reform Bill was introduced by Lord John Russell in March 1831 [7] It proposed to disfranchise the worst of the rotten boroughs and small towns (168 seats in total) which were to be given to the large towns or counties. There was to be a standard voting qualification; all occupiers of property with a rateable value of £10 a year (*the £10 householder*) were to have the vote. It was the scale of the operation which frightened people, the Tories believing that it would destroy the balance of the constitution. In Wiltshire alone, Great Bedwyn, Heytesbury, Hindon, Ludgershall, Old Sarum, Wootton Bassett and, after a struggle, Downton,[8] were to lose both MPs, while Wilton, Westbury, Malmesbury and Calne each lost one member.

Lord Grey was no believer in democracy. 'There is no one more decided against ... universal suffrage and the ballot than I am' but he saw that in the circumstances of the 1830s, reform was both expedient and necessary.[9] His thoughts were eloquently expressed by the young Thomas Macaulay in a House of Commons debate in March 1831: 'I support this measure as a measure of reform; but I support it more as a measure of conservation. That we may exclude those whom it is necessary to exclude, we must admit those whom it may be safe to admit ... the voice of great events is proclaiming to us, "Reform that you may preserve"'.[10] Grey's proposal to include the emerging middle classes was given complete backing from the 'respectable' citizens of Salisbury including Dr Richard Fowler from Milford, chemist Robert Squarey of Blue Boar Row, architect John Peniston and William Fawcett, names which crop up again and again in mid 19th century Salisbury.

In March 1831 a petition was immediately placed in the Council House (the Guildhall) for such 'respectable' city householders to show their support for the reform bill.[11] 'Respectability' was the key word, which was equated with the new industrial and commercial classes, professional men and shopkeepers. When the second reading of the bill passed by one vote the news was received with delight and the bells of the city's churches 'struck up merry peals which rang all day' and at a reform meeting, William Bird Brodie, the *Journal* editor, was asked in an open letter signed by 40 principal inhabitants to stand against Wyndham in the event of a dissolution of parliament. Brodie accepted, despite some misgivings because of his personal friendship with Wyndham. The popularity of the movement was again apparent when 170 citizens, headed by Charles Stokes and John Leach, grocers and tea dealers, wrote to the *Journal* requesting that the council should not elect a candidate who would not support the measure. When Russell's bill was then defeated in committee, a general election followed, fought entirely on the issue of reform.[12]

Of the election in the city, on 30 April 1831, the *Journal* reported that 'more interest attached to this than any other similar occurrence in living memory' and 41 of a possible 55 council members met at 11am in the crowded Great Room at the Council House with the mayor John Pinckney as the presiding officer. The candidates were the sitting members, Wyndham and Bouverie, with Brodie entering the contest for the first time.

The meeting was a stormy one with the mayor unable to keep order during the speeches from the three candidates amidst general uproar, 'the auditory being composed of all sorts, sizes and descriptions'. The *Journal* reporters noted that the noise was so dreadful that they could not hear Mr Wyndham's speech at all and only the 'odd sentence' of Mr Brodie's. The latter was accused of inconsistency because of his past friendship and support for Wyndham. During the proceedings a terrier dog was placed on the table 'to catch the rats', a possible reference to a contemporary member of the Wyndham family who was known as 'the ratcatcher'.[13] A letter from Bouverie to his brother, Lord Radnor endorsed the sense of chaos. Whilst he (Bouverie) 'escaped without harsh words ... Brodie's [supporters] had brought into the Council House a mob to back his cause and when so collected no one had any control over them'. Despite the cheers for Bouverie and Dr Fowler in their support for reform, at the close of poll the results were as follows:

Bouverie	31
Wyndham	27
Brodie	7

(and so the two existing members were returned).[14]

Bouverie further commented that despite receiving only seven votes, Brodie was 'chaired from the Market Place to his house in the Close, [while] Wyndham and his party were much hustled by the Mob in going from the Council House to his house'.[15]

But in the country as a whole the Whigs were returned by the unreformed electorate with a landslide victory and Lord John Russell introduced the Reform Bill for a second time, where it reached the House of Lords. Peers had no constituents to make them alter their views and were far less affected by pressure for change.

Brodie began to canvas support in earnest and used the medium of his paper to

Brougham Reform Cordial. This reform souvenir was found in the back garden of the *Crown and Anchor*, Exeter Street, during the construction of the Friary development. The first Baron Brougham was Lord Chancellor in Grey's Whig administration and a leading spokesman on parliamentary reform. In 1834 he stayed with the Earl of Radnor and gave a speech from the balcony of the *White Hart Hotel*. Photograph by Austin Underwood, c1960. Permission granted by the late Mary Underwood.

publicise his campaign. Endless meetings were documented at length, to such an extent that at a reform meeting at Devizes, addressed by Brodie and others, the *Journal* reporters were forced to admit that unfortunately 'our little stock of paper being here exhausted, we were not able to take notice of the speeches of ...'. Meanwhile a petition signed by 1500 citizens was sent to the sympathetic Earl of Radnor in the Lords.[16] Despite this activity, and the support for reform in the country, the Lords, on 8 October, 1831, rejected the bill by 41 votes with the majority of the bishops voting against the measure, including Thomas Burgess, Bishop of Salisbury. In response to what was seen as defying the will of the people some radical papers appeared with black edges in mourning. The *Journal* did not reach these extremes but in its leader wrote of 'the most heartfelt sorrow' and an event 'pregnant with consequences'. It was indeed, because rejection was followed by serious riots, especially in Bristol, where in the last days of October, the mob rioted for several days, 12 men were killed and the Bishop's Palace burnt down. Unrest in Yeovil and Chard led to the establishment of political unions. In Salisbury 'a large party of persons entered the Close, made a most wanton attack on the house (the Hungerford Chantry) of Mr (Daniel) Eyre', a known Wyndham supporter.[17] Painter and glazier William Small described helping his father reglaze the '60 or 70 Sash Squares [which] were smashed at Mr D Eyre's front windows'.[18] The same 'party' also broke lamps in front of Wadham Wyndham's house, the College, as well as Colonel Baker's residence in St Ann Street. The *Devizes Gazette*, a conservative paper, noted that the gates of the Close were to be shut 'at twilight, as the vengeance of the mob appears to be particularly directed against some of the residents there … the magistrates are swearing in special constables.' Several letters to the *Journal* commented on these disturbances and events were followed closely by the paper which condemned the violence but felt that the Lords had much to answer for.[19]

The Reform Bill was introduced yet again and seemed to be passing through the Lords in the early months of 1832, but the peers found a good wrecking amendment and the bill was defeated in committee stage in the first week of May.[20]

In an unprecedented action prime minister Grey asked the King to create 60 Whig peers to enable the bill to survive. William IV refused, Grey resigned on 9 May and England for a few days appeared to be without a government in the 'Days of May'. Some even thought that England was on the verge of revolution and the middle class reformers were happy to conduct a propaganda campaign that *only* reform would prevent revolution. Petitions from Salisbury were sent to the King, and the *Journal* reported feelings of 'gloomy forebodings' on the news of the prime minister's resignation. In the city 'the cause of Reform is equally if not more popular than in any other place in the kingdom'… the future was 'shadowed with clouds and thick darkness' and the editor even apologised to readers for the omission of adverts and other reports because of the political accounts.[21]

Meanwhile the news was rushed from London to the waiting crowds in the city. Under the heading *Extraordinary Despatch*, the *Journal* relayed the information that the debate in the Lords ended at 11.30pm on Monday and the express mail coach with unprecedented speed travelled 82 miles to reach Salisbury at 9.45am on the Tuesday morning with the result.[22]

These were the tensest moments in 18 months of extreme political excitement, but the Tory Duke of Wellington was unable to form an administration and in the end the King recalled Grey with the promise that he would create enough Whig peers to get the bill through the Lords and the threat proved sufficient – the Bill was passed.

When, on 21 May, the news arrived in Salisbury 'that his Majesty had sent for Earl Grey, the joy of our townsmen knew no bounds. In every part of the city there were to be seen little groups of persons congratulating each other … and the bells rang merrily all day', except St Martin's Church where the bells were afflicted 'with such a sudden hoarseness' that they were not 'once heard during the entire day'! And the *Journal* continued, 'We may truly say that *Salisbury has never in our time known a*

Chronology of the reform crisis at Westminster, 1830-1832

November 1830
    Lord Grey and the Whigs formed a government
    Whigs committed to a measure of parliamentary reform

March 1831 - First Reform Bill
    Introduced in the House of Commons by Lord John Russell
    Second reading passed by one vote
    Subsequently defeated by an amendment in committee
    Parliament was dissolved and a general election held in May 1831
    Unreformed electorate returned Grey with an overwhelming majority

June 1831 - Second Reform Bill
    Bill passed easily through the Commons; was rejected by the Lords
    Serious unrest in October/November, notably in Nottingham, Derby, and especially Bristol where the mob rioted for two days

December 1831 - Third Reform Bill
    Introduced by Lord John Russell
    Passed by the Commons but held up in the House of Lords

April/May 1832
    William IV was reluctant to create sufficient peers to ensure the bill's passage through the Lords
    Grey resigned, leading to 'the days of May'
    Wellington (Tory) unable to form a government
    The king sent for Grey and agreed to create sufficient peers to pass the bill. The threat proved sufficient
    No new peers were created and the Lords passed the bill

June 1832
    The 1832 Reform Bill became law

Procession of the Salisbury Lodge of Druids, 27 June 1832, passing along Queen Street, by G P Wainwright. © Wiltshire and Natural History Society (DZSWS:1999.1023)

happier day'. Henry Hatcher notes somewhat cynically, 'as if in celebration of some great national success'.[23]

The Reform Bill became law on 7 June 1832; a great festival of celebration was planned for 26-27 June, with a public holiday and dinner in the Market Place, paid for by general subscription. While the *Hampshire Chronicle* was both 'concerned that the plan was concocted ... in opposition to the wishes of the peaceable and well-disposed inhabitants' and that the 'crowd would be heated with beer and inflamed by the radical speeches', the organisation committee, led by John Peniston, recorded in detail the seating arrangements, subscriptions, both monetary and in kind, the programmes and processions [24] The Giant and Hob Nob were invited; the streets were covered with foliage, resembling 'an immense grove', and reform transparencies illuminated the city. Despite the *Hampshire Chronicle's* concern that the illuminations were a potential fire risk, the *Journal* filled two columns with the 'brilliance' of the occasion. The Market Place presented a 'splendid appearance'. In New Canal a transparency displayed Britannia on a rock holding a scroll with the words 'The Reform Bill'. Even the *Rose and Crown* at Harnham joined in the spirit showing an illuminated Duke of Wellington prostrate at the feet of Earl Grey.[25] There were processions led by the Ancient order of Druids, marching bands and a dinner for 2240 in the Market Place for all the male population over 14, supervised by the mayor, William Fawcett. Another 6000, (women, children under 14 and the infirm) were to be provided for in their own homes while the 'juveniles' were allowed, solely on the evening of the 27th, to let off their fireworks in the Greencroft, following rustic sports. The *Journal* proudly recorded the success of the celebrations and even Henry Hatcher was forced to admit that 'after so much excitement, not the slightest disorder occurred and the assemblage broke up, with perfect good humour and tranquility'.[26]

What did the Reform Act achieve?

Nationally, it extended the franchise a little, from 400,000 to 900,000, just one in seven of the adult male population. It largely eliminated the rotten boroughs. In Salisbury, new city boundaries were laid down to include parts of Milford and Fisherton which meant that in 1831 the population of the electoral district was nearly 12,000.[27] Of the 2336 houses in the city, 627 were valued at £10 upwards and as in the country as a whole it was the 'respectable' male, middle classes who gained the vote.

When the post-reform election took place in December 1832 there were 576 electors instead of the 41 council members who voted in 1831. 'The citizens were ... summoned,

Snuff box in the form of a coffin: Old Sarum, died 7 June 1832, aged 584. Courtesy of Salisbury and South Wiltshire Museum (SBYWM: 1934.100)

No.	Christian Name and Surname of each Voter.	Street, Lane, or other Place wherein the Property is situate.	W.	B.	Br.
		ST. EDMUND'S (CONTINUED.)			
78	Everett, Charles William	Endless-street	—		
79	Fulford, John	Castle-street	—		
80	Finch, William	Endless-street	—		—
81	Finch, Charles	Winchester-street	—		—
82	Foot, Samuel	Endless-street	—		
83	Fawcett, William	Blue-Boar-Row		—	—
84	Fitz, Thomas	Blue-Boar-Row		—	—
85	Figes, William	Winchester-street	—		
86	Fox, Charles	Milford-street	—		—
87	Foreman, Richard	Milford-street	—		—
88	Griffin, John	Castle-street		—	—
89	Griffin, William	Castle-street		—	—
90	Gregory, John	Castle-street		—	—
91	Gillingham, Richard	Milford-street		—	—
92	Gillingham, John	Milford-street		—	
93	Griffin, Thomas	Castle-street			—
94	Golborn, William	Blue-Boar-Row		—	—
95	Good, John Everitt	Endless-street			—
96	Gillingham, Samuel	Milford-street			—
97	Hetley, Henry	Endless-street	—		
98	Hatcher, Henry	Endless-street	—		
99	Hill, Stephen	Bedwin-street			—
100	Horder, James	Milford-street		—	—
101	Horder, William	Milford-street		—	—
102	Hall, Peter	Winchester-street	—		
103	Hull, Thomas	Church-street	—		
104	Harris, John	Rollestone-street		—	—
105	Hayter, William	Rollestone-street	—		—

Extract from the register of persons who voted for Wyndham, Bouverie and Brodie in December 1832, the first election following the Reform Act. This shows that while Henry Hatcher 'plumped' for anti-reformer Wyndham, the more liberal William Fawcett voted for the two reformers. Courtesy of Wiltshire and Swindon History Centre, (451/56, item xiv)

for the first time ... to exercise the important privilege of choosing fit and proper persons to represent them in Parliament'. The growth of literacy meant an increasingly well informed public and 'the city exhibited a scene of bustle and animation' in spite of unfavourable weather.[28] Brodie, Bouverie and Wyndham all stood again and as one would expect, Wyndham gained a majority in the Close, Brodie in Fisherton. The voting took place over two days and strenuous efforts were made on the final day to bring eligible electors to the hustings as Bouverie and Wyndham were neck and neck. But the final result was very different from that of 1831.[29]

Brodie	392
Wyndham	268
Bouverie	265

The reformers were disappointed at Bouverie's defeat and he was saddened because of his family's long links with the city. The 'gallant Captain (Bouverie) said ... that had he lowered himself to use the "arts" of his adverseries, then his return would have been certain'.[30] His agents queried 16 votes on the grounds that qualified voters had been excluded from the poll and the issue went before a House of Commons committee which determined in Bouverie's favour. So it was announced in May 1833 that anti-reformer Wyndham was 'not duly elected a Citizen to serve in this present Parliament for the city of New Sarum and that the Honourable Duncombe Pleydell Bouverie is duly elected'.[31] The two reformers, Brodie and Bouverie (with an additional eight votes) thus represented Salisbury in the first post-reform parliament. In the country the Whigs were swept to victory under Earl Grey.[32]

In many ways the excitement seems extraordinary because this was essentially a conservative measure to include the middle classes, but it was the first attack on the landed aristocracy and the House of Lords, and it indicated that the country was ready for change on a larger scale. Robert Peel, the future Conservative prime minister and opposed to reform in 1832, stated that he 'was unwilling to open a door which he saw no prospect of being able to close',[33] and so it proved. The 'Great' Reform Act was indeed a stepping stone to further democratic changes.

Ruth Newman is the co-author with Jane Howells, of Salisbury Past *and in 2011 they edited and transcribed* William Small's Cherished Memories and Associations, *volume 64 of the Wiltshire Record Society.*

Bibliography and Notes
Benson, R and Hatcher, H, 1843, *Old and New Sarum or Salisbury,* Nichols
Howells, J and Newman, R, 2011, eds, *William Small's Cherished Memories and Associations,* Wiltshire Record Society, 64
The History of Parliament: www.historyofparliamentonline.org, accessed 2012
Victoria History of Wiltshire (VCH)
VCH 5, 1957, Pugh, R B and Crittall E, eds
VCH 6, 1962, Crittall E, ed
Wheeler, W A, 1889, *Sarum Chronology: a brief record of the most salient events in the history of Salisbury*
Wright, D G, 1970, *Democracy and Reform 1815-1885,* Longman Group

Reform Act 1832

Records at the Wiltshire and Swindon History Centre (WSHC)
451/398 Peniston Papers, items relating to the organisation of a festival in Salisbury to celebrate the passing of the first reform bill, 1832
490/1375 Radnor Papers, letters, notices, cuttings etc relating to an election, 1831

Abbreviations

SJ =The Salisbury and Winchester Journal

Notes

1   Quoted in Cowie L W, May 1979, 'Old Sarum, a pocket borough, *History Today*, 289-296
2   Thomas Macaulay, speech in the house of Commons, March 1831, quoted in Cowie, *ibid*
3   *Potwalloper* boroughs had votes for all who owned their own house and fireplace. *Scot and lot* boroughs were similar. Here the vote was held by all male householders who paid local rates and were not on poor relief. These boroughs often had a wider franchise in the 18th century than after 1832.
4   The 1831 population of 9876 included the three city parishes and The Close. Wheeler, p53
5   *Devizes Gazette*, 15 June, 1826, p3, letter from a Salisbury 'citizen'
6   Benson and Hatcher, p570
7   As the son of a duke he could sit in the House of Commons
8   Downton was originally to lose only one of its MPs, but the radical Lord Radnor who described himself as its 'proprietor' urged its complete disfranchisement because of the potential for corruption under the leadership of a single patron – himself
9   Earl Grey, speech in the house of Lords, November, 1831
10   The most brilliant speech in defence of the Reform Bill was given by Thomas Macaulay, 2 March, 1831. Quoted in Wright, *Democracy and Reform*, p34, 117-8
11   *SJ*, 14 March, 1831, p4
12   *SJ*, 28 March, 1831, p4, 18 April, p4, 25 April, 1831, p4
13   Wyndham, H A, 1950, *A Family History*, Oxford University Press, p233
14   Each council member had the right to vote twice but some chose to 'plump' (vote only for one candidate). No one voted for Wyndham *and* Brodie. The latter's brother-in-law John Hussey came 60 miles to plump for Wyndham
15   *SJ*, 2 May, 1831, p4, WSHC 490/1375
16   *SJ*, 26 Sept, 1831, p4, 3 Oct, 1831 p4, WSHC 490/1375
17   *SJ*, 10 Oct, 1831, p4
18   Howells and Newman, p58
19   *SJ*, 10 Oct, 1831, p 4; *Devizes Gazette* 13 Oct, 1831, p3
20   The Tory peers passed an amendment which sought to postpone discussion of the disfranchisement clauses in committee. They believed that Grey would not resign over a minor, technical issue
21   *SJ*, 14 May, 1832, p4
22   *SJ*, 14 May, 1832, p4
23   *SJ*, 21 May, 1832, p4, Benson and Hatcher, p572

St Martin's church was noted for its Tory views. At least two of Wyndham's closest supporters were influential members of this church

24   *Hampshire Chronicle,* 23 June, p3; WSHC 451/398

25   The transparencies were pictures or inscriptions painted on some transparent substance, such as fabric or glass, made visible by means of a light behind, probably oil lamps. Gas lighting was not used in Salisbury until 1833.

26   *SJ,* 11 June, 1832, p4, 2 July, 1832, p3; Benson and Hatcher, p572

27   The population of the new electoral district in 1831 included the three city parishes and Close (9876) plus Fisherton (1496) and Milford (523), 11,895 in total, Wheeler, *Sarum Chronology,* p53

28   *SJ,* 17 Dec, 1832, p2

29   Taken from *A correct Register of the Persons who voted for Representatives for the City and Borough of Salisbury, in December, 1832, being the first Election which took place after the passing of the Reform Act.* Wiltshire and Swindon History Centre (451/56, item xiv)

30   *SJ,* 17 Dec, 1832, p2

31   *SJ,* 13 May, 1833, p4

32   For the first time the county of Wiltshire was divided for electoral purposes; a northern division based on Devizes and a southern division which had Salisbury as its capital, both with two seats. John Bennett of Pyt House was elected unopposed for Wiltshire south along with the Conservative Sidney Herbert, friend of Florence Nightingale and half brother to the Earl of Pembroke.

33   Sir Robert Peel in the House of Commons, 6 July 1831

Mary and George Engleheart of Dinton

Lucille H Campey

George and Mary Engleheart of Dinton were a remarkable couple. George became a famous daffodil grower, while Mary, his wife, devoted much of her life to prayer. Their personal papers, now in the Wiltshire and Swindon Record Office, reveal how they supported one another although, uncharacteristically for the late Victorian period, Mary's religious needs took precedence over George's early calling as an Anglican minister. Being born to a Quaker couple, she converted as a child to the Anglican faith and later became a Roman Catholic. Her religious journey took many twists and turns, all narrated by her daughter Catherine who, in a 75 page handwritten document, conveys something of the inner turmoil that engulfed Mary soon after her marriage to George.[1]

Born in 1855, Mary Evans was raised in a Quaker household. To the amazement and dismay of her parents she announced at the age of seven that she wished to become a Roman Catholic. According to Catherine, Mary had begun to appreciate prayers and scriptures from 'the very air she breathed ... there was something within her that knew God and could speak to him and hear his Voice and she believed that after this life she would be able to see him.'[2] But this was a Roman Catholic God. Needless to say, her parents tried to thwart her religious conversion and sent her to live with a grandmother in Edgbaston, where she could attend a Quaker school.

But, everything changed when Mary met George Engleheart. She was 17 and he was 22. Born in the Channel Islands, George was an Oxford graduate who, according to Mary, was 'very intellectual and mentally far my superior'.[3] George fell in love with her at first sight and proposed marriage, but Mary declined initially. She had long since decided that when she was old enough to leave home she would become a nun and live in a Roman Catholic convent. But when George told her how much he loved and needed her she wavered. And so the courtship began. Now 18, this 'tall, shapely girl of

Photograph of George Engleheart in later life. Wiltshire and Swindon History Centre (1498/39).

beautiful carriage'[4], as she was then, exchanged love letters, this being a sample of one of George's letters to her:

> A little while ago I was reading in the xiii [chapter] St. John and thought a great deal about the words of Our Lord to his disciple in the 34th and 35th verses. [*A new commandment I give unto you, That ye love one another; as I have loved you, that ye also love one another. By this shall all men know that ye are my disciples, if ye have love one to another.*] These words seem to give us so certain a promise that we can make our earthly love for one another Christ-like and beautiful.[5]

In their letters they exchanged descriptions of fine views, rare flowers and birds as well as passages from literature and the scriptures. And on days when they were apart they agreed the exact time when each would say the same prayer.

They married in 1878, when Mary was 23 and George was 28, and went to live in Appleshaw, to the north west of Andover. Two years later George was appointed vicar of its Anglican church and Mary provided support by playing the organ and arranging the flowers. However, she did so with growing reluctance. Seven years after marrying George, Mary found that she needed to convert to the Roman Catholic faith. Her peace of mind required it. Writing a long letter in 1884 to Cardinal John Henry Newman, who was himself a high-profile convert from the Church of England to Roman Catholicism, she revealed her dilemma: 'I must separate my soul from his; I cannot trust to his judgment and risk my soul to it any longer. If death came now I should feel only terror and dread'. She also felt isolated. Although 'outwardly happy, ... we go a great deal into society', she felt that she was 'living amongst a strange people of another religion'.[6]

Because at the time Mary needed George's permission to become a Catholic he too wrote to Cardinal Newman:

> May her husband be allowed to make known to your Eminence how entirely he honours and loves her and how fully assured he is that in taking this step she is obeying what to her is the Voice of God which she may not disregard. Nothing less could have led her whither she is gone, for her only desire and joy in life has ever been the service of God [7]

George was on her side but not her extended family. Angry cousins chastised her and so did her godfather, John Shorthouse who wrote a strongly-worded letter to George:

> If she joins the Roman heresy she will find herself awfully deceived and, she will, I have no hesitation in saying, some day bitterly regret that she the wife of an English Priest took such a step.[8]

Little Clarendon. It was granted to the National Trust by Mary Engleheart in 1940.

To add to her woes Mary was deeply troubled by the realisation that her religious conversion would require George to renounce his Anglican ministry:

> It breaks my heart to bring this trouble upon my husband ... I am 31 now and my friends can surely no longer refuse to allow me the right to have a soul of my own as they seemed to do in my girlhood. It is no pleasant path that I am choosing for myself – it involves the loss of all that is dear to me in earthly things.[9]

Nevertheless, with George's support, Mary became a Catholic in 1887. However, she was no ordinary Catholic. Her hand-written schedules appear to suggest that she wished to live like a nun, this being an example[10]:

Days when I may not attend Church		Days when I go to Church
6.30	Rise	Rise
7.30	Prime	Prime
8.00	God – before Crucifix	Mattins in church
8.30	Breakfast	Breakfast
9.00	Terce	Terce
9.15	Practise	Practise
10.00	School	School
12.00	Sexts	Sexts
12.15	Lie down	Lie down
2.00	Dine	Dine
2.30	Dress	Dress
3.00	None	None
3.15	Read in chair or write	Read in chair or write
4.30		God
5.00	Evensong read	Evensong in church
5.30	Walk	Walk
6.15	Tea	Tea
6.45	Sewing or writing	Do sewing
8.30	Undress	Undress
9.00	Compline	Compline

Meanwhile, George, having left his clerical duties behind him, decided to experiment with hybrid daffodils. Dean Herbert, a relative who was an amateur gardener, claimed to have discovered a new species of narcissus, but had failed to win backing for his achievement from his contemporaries. George set himself the task of proving him right. As Herbert had done previously, he crossed 'the wild pheasant's eye', known as

Vestiges of rows in the field behind Little Clarendon

poeticus, with the ordinary trumpet variety and waited seven years for his seedlings to flower. His patience was rewarded with the arrival of 'Horace' – his first triumph which caused a huge stir in horticultural circles. George would later name his other creations after his favourite poets, who included Horace, Virgil, and Chaucer.

His 'Will Scarlett', with its striking red cup, then went on to triumph at the Birmingham Flower Show held in 1898. Six bulbs were sold for the unprecedented sum of £100. His 'Beersheba', a white trumpet variety also won him considerable acclaim. By 1900 these successes brought him the ultimate honour of being awarded the Victoria Medal of Honour by the Royal Horticultural Society. According to a later narcissus expert, he had well and truly arrived:

Engleheart has enriched gardens with many lovely flowers with charming names. His Horace was one of the first, and I have heard him say that he would not have believed a prophet who told him that the small bed of his of this variety, which at one time contained the whole stock, could in so short a time have provided the Old and New Worlds with millions of this popular flower.[11]

George's advancement to commercial-scale gardening followed a key decision he and Mary had taken in 1901 when they bought a Tudor stone farmhouse in Dinton, now known as Little Clarendon. Costing £1,725, they spent nearly another £1000 on what was then a derelict building and moved in a year later.[12]

Both house and land were in a dreadful state. The house was divided between two families in a warren of passages and rooms like biscuit tins. The old fireplaces had to be discovered and the shape of the original rooms ... the walls were covered with patterned paper, the ceilings set to hide the old beams and half the mullion windows were built up ... and a spiral staircase in its turret was blocked up and no one seemed even aware of its existence. The walled garden was a cinder heap.[13]

Mary supervised the refurbishment of Little Clarendon while George organised the flower beds and outbuildings. Catherine noted how visitors would remark on the

Exterior of the Roman Catholic chapel

extraordinary feeling of tranquillity within the house. Was it the arrangement of the furniture, the way the light fell, the wooden panelling, the ticking of the grandfather clock or the bird song coming in from the garden? While these features contributed Catherine believed that above all, the calming influence came from 'my mother who lived and moved peacefully, always in the light of eternal things'.[14]

The 29 acres that George acquired with the house gave him the necessary space to build his many greenhouses and to plant rows of daffodils in large beds, his favourite being 'White Lady', which he grew by the acre in commercial quantities. According to Catherine, the family's workload was particularly heavy in the Spring:

> We were busy from early morning until late at night – helping to pick bunch, pack and receive visitors who came in crowds. Some came merely as a social past-time to see a pretty sight, some on earnest business My mother's hospitality was as great and all-embracing as it was magnificent. ... Even in winter there was happy sunny work in our sheltered wood ... there were whole glades of wild cyclamen and white-belled daffodils, lilies of the valley and Solomon seal which my father gave for naturalising in the wood.[15]

Meanwhile as George was wooing the world with his daffodils, Mary spent as much time as she could praying and attending services at the Roman Catholic church in Tisbury. But by 1920 she had concocted a plan that would transform her life. She had the bakery in the Little Clarendon grounds converted to a Catholic chapel, doing so while George was away in Scotland on business.

It was a chapel for public use with services being held on Sundays, but having an unusual alignment, in that the altar was on the west side.[16] Wishing to contain the costs, Mary used carved wooden pillars from a four-poster bed to embellish the altar. She also kept the east side of the bakery intact in order to allow access to an outside staircase and upper gallery, which could provide extra seating.[17] Mary's frugality was very much in evidence! In all 40 people could be accommodated. The chapel, dedicated to Our Lady of Pity, cost just over £190 and originally had its own priest – Father Rivara who held services there until 1934.[18]

The Tabernacle had particular significance for Mary since it was in here that the Sacred Host was kept. She believed that through the host she was in the very presence of Our Lord. This realisation brought her the peace of mind that she craved. But its other important function was to provide the focus for the burial ground that Mary was planning for herself and George. Thus, when George died in 1936, aged 84, he was buried in the grounds of Little Clarendon:

> My mother had his [George's] grave prepared and her own beside it in the little secret lawn against the altar end of the chapel where the beautifully carved outside crucifix looks down on them from the wall above.[19]

Interior of the Roman Catholic chapel

Of course, being buried close to the altar end of the chapel had particular significance for them both.

When George's obituary appeared in *The Times* he was described as 'well-read, highly cultured and appreciative of all that is beautiful, with a deep knowledge of the distant past and a lively interest in the present; he was a charming companion and a correspondent whose neat and clear handwriting it was always a pleasure to receive'.[20] A well-known amateur archaeologist who discovered many of the prehistoric artefacts for Dinton which have since been housed in the Devizes and Salisbury museums, George was a great authority on Stonehenge and a prominent member of the Society of Antiquaries. An article on Stonehenge appeared in *The Times* on the day before he died.[21] Meanwhile, Mary's death in 1948, at the age of 93, went largely unnoticed.[22]

George, the world-famous daffodil grower and acclaimed amateur archaeologist, acquired a high public profile while Mary's religious journey through life had been very private. She dedicated herself to attaining closeness to God through prayer. Possibly she was a mystic, although no one at the time but George and her daughter Catherine would have known this. Mary's six page letter to George from Rome describing a sermon given by Padré Agostino of Montefeltro in the church of San Carlo in Rome revealed the extraordinary passion she felt for her Catholic faith. Every word and every nuance of the sermon was lovingly described.[23] The rapturous joy she experienced in being present in the congregation shone through her words.

George and Mary Engleheart's love story is like no other. Mary was very fortunate in having married an ordained priest. George understood her religious dilemma. He realised that she had not chosen her religious vocation – it had chosen her. Very few husbands would have understood this and, even if they had understood, few could have coped. George guided Mary through her religious journey, but that was no easy task, as Catherine explained in her long essay about her mother:

> I would prefer reticence in relating intimate things concerning my parents; yet if their story is to be told at all, it has to be told in its joys and its sorrows. For that is life; it is the inter-working and reacting of two souls upon one another and the harmony which was eventually attained; that seems worthy of record and may help others.[24]

Harmony sometimes brings hidden benefits. If George had not been required to renounce his career as an Anglican minister would he have become a world-famous daffodil grower?

Dr Lucille H Campey is a historian and author of ten books on British emigration to Canada. She is the Programme Secretary of the Dinton Historical Society.

Bibliography and Notes

Wiltshire and Swindon History Centre (hereafter WSHC) 1498/29-64 Engleheart family papers

WSHC 1498/31: Letters of George Engleheart, 1874-5
WSHC 1498/33: Letters of Mary Engleheart on religious matters, c1870-87
WSHC 1498/36: Letter from Mary Engleheart to her husband, 1889
WSHC 1498/47: Notebooks with details of costs and repairs made to Little Clarendon, 1901
WSHC 1498/52: An account of the restoration of Little Clarendon by the Rev G H Engleheart and his wife recorded by their daughter, c1910-1940
WSHC 1498/58: Manuscript describing Mary Engleheart's life written by her daughter, Catherine, c1950

The image of George Engleheart is reproduced by kind permission of the Wiltshire and Swindon History Centre, all other photographs by Geoff Campey.

Notes

1   WSHC 1498/58: Catherine refers only briefly to her brother Paul, who was born in 1879, a year after George and Mary married. Catherine was born 18 years later. Paul died tragically in 1936 in a boating accident while in Mexico.

2   *Ibid,* pp 1-11

3   WSHC 1498/33: Mary to Cardinal Newman, October, 1884

4   WSHC 1498/58, p22

5   WSHC 1498/31: George to Mary, 22 June 1874

6   WSHC 1498/33: Mary to Cardinal Newman, October 1884

7   WSHC 1498/33: George to Cardinal Newman, 2 April 1887

8   *Ibid,* John Henry Shorthouse to George Engleheart, 3rd Sunday in Lent, 1887

9   *Ibid,* Mary to her cousin Sarah, 4 March 1887

10 WSHC 1498/33

11 E A Bowles, 1934, *Handbook of Narcissus,* Martin Hopkinson

12 WSHC 1498/47

13 WSHC 1498/52

14 WSHC 1498/58, p72

15 WSHC 1498/58, p53

16 The chapel was part of the Roman Catholic parish of Tisbury.

17 WSHC 1498/47. Five hundred Dinton bricks were used in the chapel's construction.

18 *Ibid.* A further £66 was spent in 1921 on various items for the chapel including a Tabernacle, a statue of the Virgin Mary, a Chalice, a crucifix of teak wood and candlesticks.

19 WSHC 1498/58, p74

20 *The Times,* 1936, 25 March, p21, letter from unnamed correspondent; 18 March, p16, obituary; 14 March, p13-14, Stonehenge article

21 A list of articles published by George can be found on the British and Irish Archaeological Bibliography website, www.biab.ac.uk

22 Mary suffered from dementia in her final years

23 WSHC 1498/36: Mary to George, 1889

24 WSHC 1498/58, p74

The Belle Vue estate, an early 20th century suburb

Andrew Minting

The city of Salisbury accommodated its growth at the end of the 19th century in modest suburbs on all sides, and one of the largest of these, Wyndham Park, has been described by Jane Howells in issue 7 of Sarum Chronicle (*SC7*). One significant block of land sold by the Wyndhams in 1871 passed in 1878 to the owner of Belle Vue House at the top of Endless Street, in whose ownership it remained undeveloped until the 20th century. This study looks at the architectural detail and variety of the houses in this small estate, and how it is possible to trace the sequence of development of this area and its occupants using early Ordnance Survey mapping, records created by the local building control bylaws, and trade directories.

The estate lies on the northern side of the medieval city boundary and the parish of St Edmund's, and has two streets, Albany Road and Belle Vue Road. Belle Vue House, a large early 19th century villa now converted to offices, stands between the site and Castle Street to the west, and is one of the largest and earliest of its kind in the city. The land to the south and east of the estate comprises the churchyard of St Edmund's and the open space of Wyndham Park, with Wyndham Road to the north. This block of land is clearly defined on the 1845 tithe map of the rural parish of Milford and is situated on a gentle slope rising from Castle Street in the west to London Road in the east. The tithe apportionment papers show that the land was held by the trustees of Wadham Wyndham under a lease from the Duke of Hamilton, and that it was occupied by Mary Butler as private garden.[1]

The sale of the Wyndham's lands in 1871 is described by Helen Wilcockson in *SC7*. In 1878 the Ecclesiastical Commissioners resold the site of this study, identified by the same number as on the tithe map and estimated to cover an area of six acres and three roods, to Richard Henry Rigden for £1,500. The transcribed indenture also described the land as 'Swayne's Garden'.[2] The 1900 revision of the Ordnance Survey shows

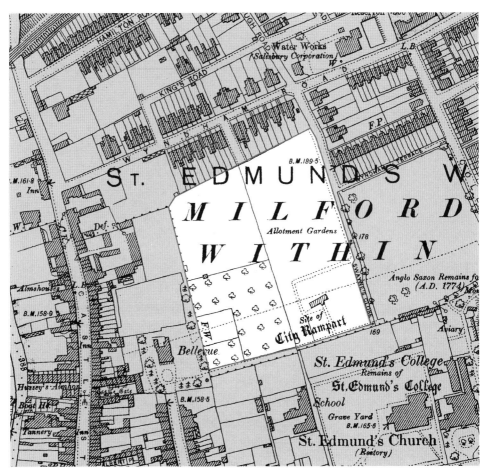

Extract from Ordnance Survey map published 1901, revised 1900. Nearly all of the land within the railway line has now been developed except for the Belle Vue Estate site.

an orchard and allotments enclosed by the completed Wyndham Park estate, and in 1904 the city boundary was redrawn to include that part of Milford known as Milford Within, including the Belle Vue estate.[3] Rigden, who had been mayor in 1864-5, died in 1885 and it was not until 1908 that his trustees put the land up for sale, this time clearly with the intention of development: a road was in the process of being constructed to the east of Endless Street along the parish boundary. The land was purchased by a group including George John Main (corn merchant), Gerald Billett (builder), Sidney Frank Musselwhite (builder), and William James Trethowan (solicitor) for £4,500.

The plan accompanying the 1908 sale shows that suburban development had already occurred to the north and east of the site, with this section of Wyndham Road complete,

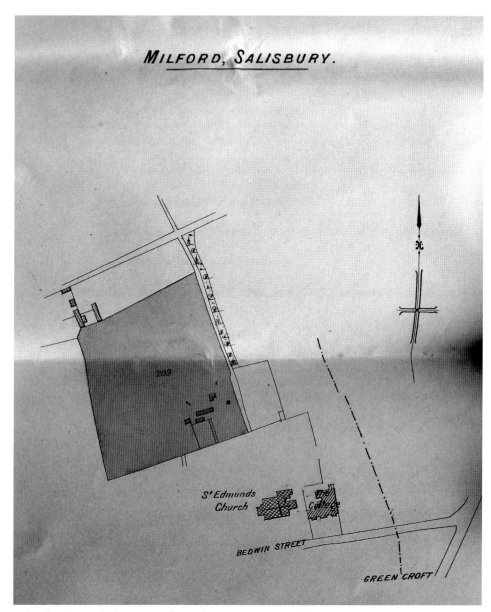

Tithe Plot 209 in sale documents of 1878. (WSHC G23/150/146)

and Swayne's Close running along the eastern boundary. The development of Belle Vue can be traced in further detail by a collection of local authority records: notifications to the Salisbury Corporation for proposed buildings under local bylaw 93. These provide

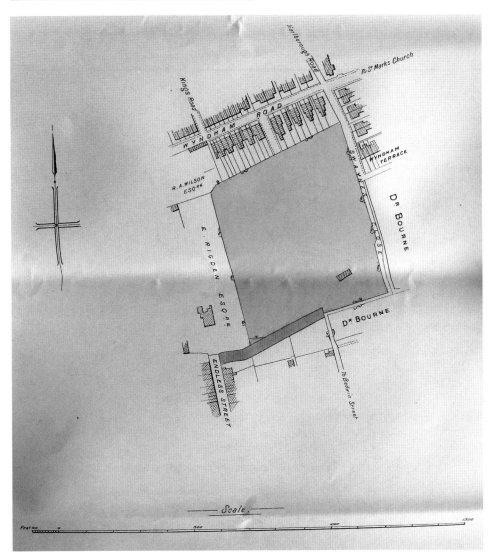

As shown in sale documents of 1908. (WSHC G23/150/146)

information including the dates of application and approval, original builder, architect, design, ceiling heights and other regulated features particularly regarding drainage (perhaps historic Salisbury's most persistent issue) and are available for many of the properties in the estate.[4] Dates of the final certification of the site by the city surveyor are often handwritten on to the approved plans. There are some notable omissions, and these appear to pre-date 1910, the year when the first of these records are available in this area, including the two grandest detached houses, 43 Albany Road (Roslin) and 75 Belle Vue Road (Fairstowe); this is confirmed by the location of their listing in the

24 Belle Vue Road. Note the absence of a window above the door

registers of the Inland Revenue's Record of Valuations prepared in 1910, thus dating their construction between 1908 and 1910.[5] These registers were updated over the following few years, and list many of the future addresses as 'building site', showing outlines of all properties on the eastern side of both roads, 3-33 Belle Vue Road and 45-57 Albany Road. The absence of any details for the land north of 33 Belle Vue Road suggests a cut-off date no later than 1915. A few future plots on the western side of Albany Road are also marked, without plans, presumably before finalisation of their details.

All houses were built of brick under a Welsh slate roof, in common with contemporary developments throughout most of the country, and incorporate copious amounts of precast reconstituted stone for window and door detailing.

The provision of the new access road, which became Belle Vue Road, linking Endless Street to Wyndham Road,[6] also facilitated development to the south of the site, and numbers 18 to 36 slightly pre-date the rest of the development. Numbers 2 to

76 Belle Vue Road. Two storeyed square bay, simple Classical detailing.

14 are much later and are described at the end of the section on Albany Road. These terraced houses (18-36) have paired front doors, very shallow projecting square two-storey bays, paired sash windows and are the only houses in the estate with no window above the front doors; reconstituted stone lintels and window mullions are decorated with rosettes and elegant forms and detailing. The gabled dormers over the bays have roughcast panels and attractive bargeboards. Numbers 3 to 7, at the southwestern end of the street, use the same prefabricated stone details for the front doors, but have a window above them.

The houses on the eastern side of Belle Vue Road appear to have been the next to be developed, with applications from local builders, Messrs Smith & Bundy, between 1910 and 1912 to build a few at a time.[7] From the certification dates, it would appear that the houses were roughly completed in pairs. Architectural drawings were provided by Alfred C Bothams, of Bothams & Brown architectural practice of Salisbury, and the houses appear to be of one design, except for the northernmost pair which is slightly wider to make use of the remaining plot and can accommodate a different plan: 88 has four bedrooms, three reception rooms and seven fireplaces. This terrace, which has a break for an access path after the first block of four houses, is otherwise unbroken at the roofline: passageways at ground floor level provide larger bedrooms for every fourth house thereafter. Two storey square bays, deeper than those above, three bedrooms, five fireplaces and upstairs bathrooms provide comfortable living.

The western side of the road is less consistent in its development, as can be seen from the map shaded by builder.(Figure 8) There is the work of four different builders between 9 and 49, with the portion to the south of 35 developed between 1912 and 1916 by Charles Stevens, Frank Bath and Messrs Smith & Bundy.[8] Bath, nephew of local architect Fred Bath, but working from Camberley, originally applied in 1912 to build 15-25, however in 1913 Messrs Smith & Bundy reapplied with amended plans for 23 and 25, providing three bedrooms and six fireplaces. They later revised plans in 1922 for 27-37 to reduce the number of dwellings and site width, amending the approved 1916 plans for 31 and 33 to make them a pair. As with several of the plans, the front bay window and dormer are not shown in the sectional drawing provided, despite appearing on the plan; unusually however, 27 and 29 are the only houses in the estate that have no dormers. Their ground floor angled bays might have provided the cheapest aggrandisation.

Number 35 is an oddity. Originally proposed by Smith & Bundy and approved as a site for terraced housing in 1916, it was revised to a larger detached house in 1925 and certified the same year.[9] This house, the only detached building between terraces in the estate, presents a very different aspect to the street, and has roughcast render to the first floor, as well as a unique plan, again by Bothams.

Numbers 37-49 were also applied for, approved and certified in 1925. Local builders W Roles & Son proposed a design that would provide four bedrooms and an upstairs bathroom, seven fireplaces, an angled ground floor bay with a parapet, and a gabled dormer.[10] The absence of an architect's name on Roles' applications implies that they were providing a design and build service, however comparison with signed drawings in the same collection suggests that they may have been provided by the local office of Lemon and Blizard, a regional practice of surveyors, architects and civil engineers, or at least, their draughtsman.

Along the northernmost part of Belle Vue Road, where it turns the corner to make its way out to Wyndham Road, stands a terrace of seven houses; these are of nearly identical detail to 37-49, and are clearly by Roles. The window mullions and lintels have minutely different detail, along with minor variation to the infill panels in the dormer gables, but the impression is one of identical housing. At each end of this row stand detached houses, albeit linked by garages to the terrace; these have terracotta detailing,

45 Albany Road by Roles. Decorative
lintels and a pierced parapet on the
bay.

projecting windows throughout and are much larger than the terraced houses. The
highest plot of the estate is occupied by what must, from its extravagant detail, be one
of its most expensively built properties; known as Fairstowe, its builder and architect
unknown, it commands views over the rooftops of the estate towards the city and the
cathedral.

To the west of the northernmost terrace just described, across the exit from Albany
Road to Wyndham Road, stands another terrace of seven houses of nearly identical
design. These have more decorative parapet detailing, door lintels and tile-hung dormer
gables, and a terra cotta string course. The general design is essentially the same for
the rest of the properties in Albany Road, minus the parapet, the differences being that
those on the east side have round-arched porches instead of gently cambered; dormer
gable infill panels roughcast with applied timbers and finials instead of roughcast with
a central brick detail lozenge; and the ground floor bay windows have a pitched lead
roof rather than flat. All of the houses in Albany Road appear to have been built by
Roles & Son between 1910 and 1916, starting on the east side, possibly earlier than the
plans show as the 1910 application relates to those in the middle of the terrace and work
almost certainly started at the southern end.[11]

38 Albany Road by Roles. Arched door head and angled bay with lead roof.

Number 43 is a very generously proportioned detached house in the northwestern corner of the estate, and was one of the first houses constructed, shown on the Valuation Office's plan in the occupation of Gerald Billett, one of the developers of the estate. To the south of 43, a pair of houses perhaps rather ambitiously described as 'semi-detached villas' on plans for Mr T W Berry by James Cleland, architect of Salisbury, were approved in May 1912 but never built; these would have included the highest documented ground floor ceilings of the estate, at nine feet, and a '2-ply ruberoid dpc' [damp proof course], but more significantly, would have presented a gable to the road rather than eaves broken with a dormer.[12]

Number 2 at the southeastern end of the road, is much wider than a single dwelling and has an internal lobby with two doors set at an angle to each other. Despite much alteration, it is clear that this building originated as a shop, (which finally closed in the early 1980s) as there are vestiges of shopfront lintels visible in the domesticated south and west elevations. Number 1 is a detached house that appears to be the only one of a row of four proposed that was constructed, and was certified in 1915.[13] Like 35 Belle Vue Road, its first floor is roughcast.

To the south of the end of Albany Road, across Belle Vue Road, the plot outside of

Housebuilders, (see key for code).

OS map published 1925, surveyed 1923. All but a small part of the Belle Vue Estate has now been developed.

the tithe award area, and separate from its changes of ownership, was finally developed as 2 to 14 Belle Vue Road between 1926 and 1928, also by Roles, but to a much more artistically elegant design. The jettied dormers, a revision of 1927, were also roughcast, while a broad timber-arched porch swept across the paired doorways under a canopy, saving on internal porch space.[14]

The houses by Roles are all named, with a carved stone nameplate at chest height by the front doors. These appear to be names often seen in residential suburbs of this period, used to bring a less ordered and more exclusive and personal impression of a development, but further investigation may prove otherwise! Very few properties have gained a name since, and only a handful have had theirs removed in some way. Fairstowe has been known as 'The Old Rectory' since it was purchased by the church in the 1950s and subsequently resold.[15]

Having apparently established the dates of construction from Corporation documents, another valuable source of information can assist in verification of this, namely trade directories. Directories for Salisbury provide both an alphabetical list of residents and a list of residents by street and occupation. Thus, it is possible to establish approximate dates of first occupation of many properties, and to learn something of the people who lived there.

These lists of occupants and occupations show that there was a wide variety in the skills of the residents. The shop at 2 Albany Road was first occupied by J E Scammell, baker and grocer, who had moved from 88 Castle Street, and several other early occupants are described as manager or clerk in 1912. Dairyman Mr Lywood purchased 3 Belle Vue Road in 1911 with the help of a £300 mortgage from the Salisbury First Perfect Thrift Building Society, a facility in its national infancy, and was succeeded by Messrs W E & H Hale (who had a smaller mortgage of £133 10s) of the Castle Dairy in 1920.[16]

Fairstowe's first householder was William Ensley Hill, his address given as Swayne's Close until 1913, having moved in by 1911 from 46 Wyndham Road almost immediately to the north; by 1923 he had been succeeded by Hedley Annetts, a china merchant operating from 35 Silver Street, who became mayor in 1953.

By 1913, Mr I J Hobden had moved into 43 Albany Road, the only house completed on this side of the street. Numbers 34-50 had new occupants, including a schoolmaster, dentist's secretary, insurance agent, postman and gardener. Of these nine houses, the residents of eight of them had moved from within the city, as confirmed with reference to earlier directories, and six from within the Wyndham Park estate. Mrs Acquier had even moved from 34 Belle Vue Road. As Belle Vue Road had been partially developed by the 1912 directory, it is harder to trace its occupants through the county directories where residents are listed alphabetically by town, however, it is still apparent that the majority of residents had moved from within the Wyndham Park estate, from Hamilton Road and St Mark's Avenue. Perhaps this was simply because of the convenience of Belle Vue, within level walking distance of the town centre where shopping and work would largely be performed. In some cases it is easy to establish the proximity between home and work, such as the Fry households, whose bakery at 35 Bedwin Street was on the doorstep; or Mr G E Pinder, of Jenkins & Pinder ironmongers on Winchester Street.

Ten years later (1923), when most of the estate was built (only 35-49 Belle Vue Road were outstanding), the spread of occupations had widened further, and included more lower middle class roles, including a civil servant, an accountant, a builder, a petrol

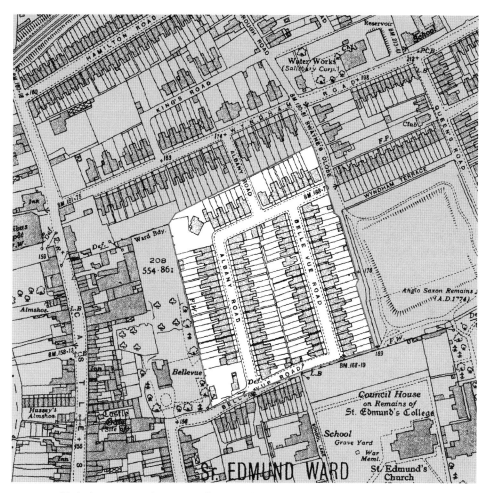

OS map published 1937, revised 1936-7. Belle Vue fully developed.

wholesaler, a member of the Royal Artillery Pay Corps and a solicitor's clerk. More manual roles also appeared, including hairdresser, carpenter, labourer, railwayman, and wheelwright; while some others are simply interesting for the period, such an electrician, a switchboard operator, trained nurse, assistant overseer of the poor, music teacher and yeast merchant.

Widows appear in Belle Vue in small numbers at this time: several ladies appear as 'Mrs' in the directory for each year; a few were widowed between the directories inspected, such as Mrs Grist of 32 Albany Road whose husband Frank died in 1915, and Mrs C Deall whose husband Edward died in 1921. Directory entries are imperfect too, giving Mrs Stinton (probably widow of Edwin, 1842-1915, of 29 Bourne Avenue) as Stirton, and widowed Mrs Bowring (probably of Thomas, 1837-1914, of 37 Rampart Road) who had her sister Ethel living with her; Ethel had married Hermann Schwender in 1911, and she predeceased him in 1937, so it remains to be discovered why she was living with her sister in 1923.[17] Alfred Callaway of Earlsfield, 55 Albany Road, died in September 1915 and his widow Catherine was granted probate a month later, with his effects valued at £725.[18]

From the record set of plans submitted to the Corporation in the period, it is also possible to learn more of the work of the builders and architects involved with the estate. None of them except A C Bothams and Lemon & Blizard is listed in Wiltshire Buildings Record's directory, *Architects and Building Craftsmen with work in Wiltshire*, and more research into the work of these firms could add to our understanding of the nature of estate development in the city. Thus we can see that Smith & Bundy continued to develop small clusters of houses at a time, and probably only in Salisbury, with approximately 45 schemes recorded until 1938. The latest dated plan from Roles and Sons was in 1933, and they had submitted 25 applications since 1910.[19] There are no other plans provided by Frank Bath or Charles Stevens in the catalogue. It also appears from inspection of the catalogue that it could also be used to look at other areas of contemporary development from 1907 onwards, particularly the estate between Downton Road and Britford Lane, the land to the east of Castle Road, and that around Bouverie Avenue.

The minimal variety of house form in the estate, with three of the four main road lengths developed in a single style, allows little room for social differentiation through variety. There are one and two storey bays, and single storey rear lean-tos to accommodate external privies and coal instead of longer rear wings, and an interesting variety of precast window and lintel details, but these are fairly minor distinctions, and on travelling through the estate one senses its pleasantly unified and tranquil character, clearly distinct from Endless Street and Wyndham Road. There is little differentiation in ceiling heights, with the overwhelming majority being 8 feet throughout, while the number of fireplaces does vary slightly but with most bedrooms heated there were no significant variations of living conditions. It is interesting to note that very little external alteration of any of these buildings has taken place since they were built: the plan is so efficient in its use of the land while providing amenity space for the occupants, that there is virtually nowhere that an extension could be built; nor is there likely to be a need – those with aspirations of upward social mobility may have sought the villas or semi-detached houses of the outer fringes of the city, at Bouverie Avenue, Paul's Dene and Milford Hill instead.

The Belle Vue Estate was built speculatively, as one would expect for such uniform and multiple developments, and seems to have been sufficiently attractive that it housed principally people of lower middle or working class status who, far from escaping the perils of an industrial city slum, were moving back towards the centre of the city from the fringes which had been developed earlier.

There is no claim that this is an exceptional suburb; houses of similar design, materials and period to the terraced housing of Belle Vue can be seen in virtually every town in England, However the development from private garden to housing, and its prior exclusion from surrounding schemes, together with the range of records available mean that an in-depth analysis of this aspect of Salisbury's suburban development has been possible.

Andrew Minting has worked as a conservation officer in Salisbury since 2005 and has recently completed his MSc in English Local History at the University of Oxford, for which an earlier version of this paper was submitted as coursework. He is also a parish church organist and lives in the Bourne valley.

Bibliography and Notes

At the Wiltshire and Swindon History Centre (WSHC)

1214/130	Tithe Map and documents for Milford, 1845
A1/210/154/EA 74	Milford Enclosure Award, 1800
G23/760	Building Regulations Bylaws: Applications and Plans
G23/150/146	Title documents for 3 Belle Vue Road

Crittal, Elizabeth, (ed), 1962, *Victoria County History, Volume 6 (VCH 6)*
Browns Directory of Salisbury and district (1912, 1913, 1923)
Hart, Peter H L, 2002, Dates of Salisbury and Wilton Streets, privately published
Kelly's Directory of Salisbury and neighbourhood, 1927
Kelly's Directory of Wiltshire, 1907, 1911
Slocombe, P (ed), 1996, *Architects and Building Craftsmen with work in Wiltshire*, Wiltshire Buildings Record
Slocombe, P (compiler) 2006, *Architects and Building Craftsmen with work in Wiltshire Part 2*, Wiltshire Buildings Record

Notes

1   WSHC 1214/130
2   WSHC G23/150/146
3   *VCH 6* (1962), pp 90-93
4   WSHC G23/760
5   WSHC L8/163-5
6   Hart: Salisbury City Council General Purposes Committee named Albany Road on 20 Oct

1910. At the same meeting they decided that the western part of Belle Vue Road, originally considered as an extension of Endless Street (meeting 21 Nov 1907), should be given its present name.

7   WSHC G23/760/28 (1910), G23/760/47 (1911), G23/760/78 (1912)

8   WSHC G23/760/71 and 78

9   WSHC G23/760/320

10   WSHC G23/760/307

11   WSHC G23/760/26

12   WSHC G23/760/70

13   WSHC G23/760/120

14   WSHC G23/760/226

15   http://www.theoldrectory-bb.co.uk/facilities.html accessed 04/05/11

16   WSHC G23/150/146

17   www.ancestrylibrary.co.uk accessed 04/05/2011; *Brown's Directory of Wiltshire*, 1923

18   National Probate Calendar (Index of Wills and Administrations),1861-1941

19   WSHC G23/760, various

The Salisbury Domesday Books: a note

Steven Hobbs and John Chandler

The purpose of this note is to draw to researchers' attention a particularly rich source for the history of medieval Salisbury which, although by no means ignored by previous historians, remains little known and has not in our view been given anything like the attention its importance deserves.[1]

The Salisbury Domesday Books, so-called by their creators and contemporaries, are four large parchment volumes (measuring 30cm by 40cm). Each one is titled Domesday followed by a series number *Liber Tertius*, *Liber Quintus*, *Liber Sextus* and *Liber Septimus*. They contain full copies of deeds and wills, first proved in the court of the Subdean of Sarum, relating to property within the city for the years 1361-1433, 1459-1479, approved and enrolled in the court of the bishop of Sarum.[2]

Why were these registers compiled and what makes them an important source for the history of the city and its citizens? Under the royal charter of 1227, and an agreement between the bishop (in his secular position as the seigneurial lord of Salisbury) and the city made in 1306, the bishop's right to collect a tax known as tallage from property owners within Salisbury was established.[3] The agreement makes reference to the register called by the citizens Domesday, indicating that it already existed, possibly since 1227. It arose from the need for the bishop to be aware of and approve changes in ownership, so that citizens liable to tallage would be known.

Book 6 has an index covering the years 1317-1422, arranged chronologically, which covers Books 1, 2, and 4 (all no longer extant), Books 3, 5, and part of Book 6 (to fol 75r). This index states the type of document, the year, names of parties, and description of properties conveyed or devised. The number of documents in the seven books is about 2,400. Of these about 1,120 survive as enrolled copies, the rest only as brief descriptions in the index. Of these documents 487 are wills, of which 182 are enrolled copies, the rest are only recorded in the index.

The title of the index (in Latin) describes it as a calendar of all the deeds, wills and other memoranda enrolled in the book called Domesday in the city of Salisbury. It covers the years 1317-1433, with gaps between 1322-1332, and 1345-1354, the latter was probably due to the hiatus caused by the Black Death. The comprehensiveness suggested in its title is certainly supported by a comparison with the contents of the extant Book 3. A typical example of an entry in the index, for a deed in one of the missing books is as follows: 1411-12 *Carta Matilda uxor Willelmi Gys facta Willelmo Sloghe de tenementi in Gigorstret* ('Grant by Matilda, wife of William Gys, to William Sloghe of a tenement in Gigant Street').[4]

The average number of documents enrolled during the 96 years is about 25. The gap of 26 years between Books 6 and 7 coincided with the episcopacy of William Ayscough when relations between bishop and city broke down (1438-1450). Fewer documents were enrolled in Book 7 (93 including only two wills for a period of 20 years), suggesting a decline in the effectiveness of the arrangement.

In more detail the contents and scope of the Books are as follows:

Book 1 (index only), 1317-1322, several undated wills, 1332-1335, 31 wills 1338-nd, and two writs 1339, 1345 making a total of c360 documents .

Book 2 (index only), 1354-1361, c270 documents. The latter part of the gap is probably due to the hiatus of the Black Death, from 1350.

Book 3, 1361-1368, 290 documents in index and register, (G23/1/212). The meetings of the court are noted in this book only, and on average about six documents were enrolled at each session.

Book 4 (index only), 1369-1395/6 c700 documents

Book 5, 1396-1413, c150 documents (G23/1/213)

Book 6, 1413-1433, 587 documents (G23/1/214)

Book 7, 1459-1479, 93 documents (G231/215)

Numbers of wills (index only): Book 1, 160; Book 2, 32; Book 4, 113. Total 305.

Numbers of wills (enrolled copies): Book 3, 52; Book 5, 22; Book 6, 95, Book 7, 2. Total 182.

Book 3 has a note (in Latin) recording the appointment on 15 September 1361 of William Dunkyrton as clerk of the city.[5] He appears frequently in the book as the final name in the witness lists of enrolled deeds described as *cler*[ico]; the position always occupied by the writer when he is identified. In Book 5 William Loord occupies the same position in many witness lists between 1396 and 1405, when Stephen Edyngton's name also appears; his election as clerk is recorded in November 1404 in the first Salisbury Ledger Book.[6] That entry is partially illegible, but it seems likely that he joined Loord,

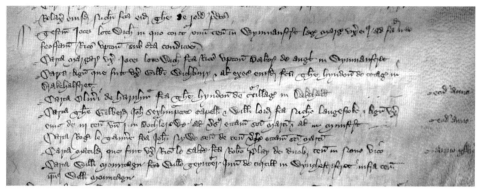

A section of the index to the Salisbury Domesday Books, listing deeds (generally beginning 'Carta') and a will (beginning 'Testamentum'). Courtesy of Wiltshire and Swindon History Centre.

indicating an increase in clerical work. They both witnessed deeds throughout the years covered by Book 6 although never together. They are important in relation to the Domesday Books because it is likely that their duties included enrolling the documents into the registers, and they may even have written many of the original deeds (see above). Comparison of the hands found in the registers and original deeds would throw light on the business of record keeping in medieval Salisbury.

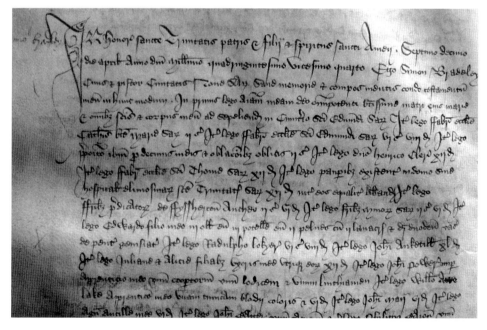

Copy, enrolled in a Domesday book, of part of the will of a Salisbury baker, Simon Bradeley, made in 1424. Courtesy of Wiltshire and Swindon History Centre.

The advantage to the parties of the deeds of enrolment was the use of the seals of the mayor and city, which strengthened authentication of the transactions. The mayor and coroner together with the bishop's bailiff appear in the witness lists of many of the deeds. Many original deeds of Salisbury properties have the seals of mayor and city attached confirming the arrangements found in the Books; one example of an original document that was copied is an extant deed of 1418 in the archives of Trinity Hospital, which is enrolled in Book 6.[7]

Collections of enrolled deeds associated with borough courts survive for many towns and cities, and have long attracted the attention of students interested in medieval law and local government.[8] In London the series created by the Court of Hustings begins in 1252, and on a more modest scale Wallingford has preserved a roll from 1231-2. Most survivors, however, begin after 1300, such as the registers kept at Bristol, King's Lynn, Lincoln, Scarborough and elsewhere, so that in this respect Salisbury's Domesday Books conform to the pattern.

The potential of such records, and other accumulations of deeds and wills, for unravelling medieval urban topography has been explored during the last 50 years in a number of distinguished studies – of Oxford, Canterbury, Bristol and, most exhaustively, Winchester.[9] For these cities it has been possible to trace the tenurial history of individual landholdings and tenements to provide a virtual street directory, which can then be linked to other documentary sources and archaeological investigations to build up a picture of medieval town development. Derek Keene, in introducing his survey of Winchester, suggested in 1985 that it would be fruitful to apply his methods to other places (he cites Norwich and London as possibilities), a suggestion taken up by Roger Leech at Bristol.[10]

Salisbury, lying between Winchester and Bristol and rapidly eclipsing the former to rival the latter, would seem an obvious candidate for similar treatment. And the transactions described by the Domesday Books, during the century building up to the city's era of greatest prosperity and pre-eminence, would undoubtedly provide a key element in such a study.

To a limited extent this has already been attempted. The RCHM inventory of city buildings used these and other contemporary medieval documents to elucidate the building history of tenements on which pre-Victorian structures have (or have until recently) survived.[11] There exist in print, also, two probably comprehensive lists of Salisbury householders, for the years 1399 and 1455. The former, although it gives no addresses other than wards, appears to be topographically arranged, since some trades are concentrated together, and one entry adds the note *in alia parte vici* (in another part of the street).[12] The latter includes many street names but is not arranged in an obviously consistent order.[13] A fourth, most important, source of information about

Salisbury people and places during its economic heyday is the recent edition of the earliest city ledger.[14]

Using these four readily available sources as reference points, it should be possible to locate many of the property transactions described in the Domesday Books and so to work towards a rudimentary street directory and prosopography[15] of Salisbury's medieval inhabitants. The researcher would be helped by the peculiar topography of the city, whereby locations may be described by street, chequer, parish or ward (or any combination), and even by 'corner'. The ease of listing, sorting and searching using a computer database, a facility not available to those working on similar studies in the past, would also be of considerable help.

The potential of the Salisbury Domesday Books, therefore, as providing much of the raw material for a directory of the medieval city, is considerable. And the value of such a study would extend well beyond academic interest in Salisbury's medieval economy, topography and society; it would also help to inform planners and archaeologists concerned with investigating development sites in future, and with interpreting the results of archaeological excavations.

Steven Hobbs, an archivist with Wiltshire Council for over 20 years, is joint general editor of the Wiltshire Record Society, for which he has edited volumes on glebe terriers and gleanings from parish registers.

Notes

1   The Domesday Books, now in the Wiltshire and Swindon History Centre (WSHC), are described in Hatcher, H,1843, *Old and New Sarum or Salisbury*, 87; Historic Manuscripts Commission, 1907, *Various Collections* 4, 191 (nos 2-3); Rathbone, M G (ed), 1951, *List of Wiltshire borough records ...* , 63-4, 80 (no 145); RCHM, 1980, *Ancient and historical monuments in the city of Salisbury*, 1, HMSO, xxvi

2   WSHC G23/1/212-215

3   WSHC G23/0/1; G23/1/222

4   Contractions have been extended.

5   The wording is '*recepit officiu' clerical' civitat' Nove Sar'*

6   WSHC G23/1/1, published in Carr, D R (ed), 2001, *The first general entry book of the city of Salisbury, 1387-1452*, Wiltshire Record Society 54

7   WSHC 1446/1/55; cf WSA G23/1/214 p71

8   Martin, G H, 'The registration of deeds of title in the medieval borough', in Bullough, D H, and Storey, R L (eds), 1971, *The study of medieval records: essays in honour of Kathleen Major*, Oxford, 151-73. Examples cited in this paragraph derive from Martin's paper.

9   Salter, H E, *Survey of Oxford*, Oxford Historical Society, new series 14, 1960; 20, 1969; Urry, W,

1967, *Canterbury under the Angevin kings,* Athlone Press; Leech, R H, 1997, *The topography of medieval and early modern Bristol,* 1, Bristol Record Society 48; Keene, D, 1985, *Survey of medieval Winchester,* 1, Oxford: Winchester Studies 2; see also Morgan, R, 1992, *Chichester: a documentary history,* Phillimore

10   Keene 1985, 442

11   RCHM, 1980.

12   Transcribed in Chandler, J, 1983, *Endless Street: a history of Salisbury and its people,* Hobnob Press, 257-72; note entry 504 and the sequence 877-898: including ironmongers, butchers and 'fyssheres' (fishmongers).

13   Nevill, E R, 1911, 'Salisbury in 1455', *Wiltshire Archaeological and Natural History Society Magazine* 37, 66-91

14   Carr, 2001

15   In this context a summary of the principal facts known about an individual (literally a 'facebook').

Sunshine or gloom - the Victorian glazing in the Salisbury Chapter House

Keith Blake

Early in 1967, the Chapter of Salisbury Cathedral found themselves in the news in a way that most of them probably did not relish. Articles appeared in the local papers and in *The Times*. A question was asked in the House of Lords. There were hints of a rift within the Chapter, and sub editors enjoyed themselves with headlines such as 'Chapter saw through their glass darkly' and 'The Canon of Barchester'. The cause of this predictable evocation of the world of Anthony Trollope was a decision to remove the Victorian windows from the Chapter House and the subsequent reversal of this decision. This paper examines the background to these events, and tries to explore how far they reflected contemporary attitudes to conservation.

The Chapter House escaped Wyatt's 18th century reordering of the Cathedral and by 1800 its structure was showing signs of neglect. Over the next 50 years any remaining 13th century glass in its eight large windows was gradually removed and re-sited elsewhere in the cathedral.[1] This included the heraldic shields described by David Richards in issue 11 of *Sarum Chronicle*.[2] Initial replacement was with pieces of clear glass (quarries) set in lead. In 1861, as part of Henry Clutton's restoration, Messrs Ward and Hughes installed windows with a variety of coloured geometric patterns.[3]

During the 1960s the future of these windows came under discussion. in May 1964, the Canon Treasurer told the Chapter that 'it was proposed to reglaze the windows of the Chapter House with clear leaded glass in place of the present monotonous and cheap Victorian glass …The Clerk of Works said that he would be glad of the opportunity to restore the stone mullions and window frames as these were now in poor condition.' The Clerk of Works was authorised to start work on 6 January 1965 and the Chapter House was to be closed while work was in progress.[4]

What happened in January 1965 is not clear. According to a letter[5] sent in 1967 from

The north window, with original Ward and Hughes glazing

the Dean (K W Haworth) to *The Times*:

> in the course of normal maintenance we began to treat two windows, replacing them with clear glass, on local advice and with the encouragement of many who, using the Chapter House for conference, said they found this particular glass oppressive.

But, as we have seen, in 1964 the Chapter had been told that the windows should in any case be reglazed, and that maintenance would be merely a matter of opportunity, and so already recollections were shifting. Rumours apparently began to circulate. An article published in 1967 in the *Architects' Journal*[6] (under the heading 'The Canon of Barchester') said that some 'friends of the Cathedral' remembered seeing 'a suspicious notice' outside the Chapter House and suspected 'a clandestine act of destruction' was being perpetrated.

These fears may have been fuelled by memories of an earlier removal. In May 1965 *The Times* reported allegations by Mrs Ann Crosley of Salisbury that 'good representations of Victorian workmanship' had been destroyed. She mentioned the Victorian glass in the Chapter House, and a screen. In 1873 Sir George Gilbert Scott had designed, and Francis Skidmore had built, an elaborate painted wrought iron screen to separate the nave from the chancel. This screen had been removed as part of a major reordering of the Sanctuary, overseen by the architect partners Seeley and Paget, in 1959/60.[7] The screen had disappeared 'literally overnight',[8] and it doubtless did not help that, after a long search to find it a new home, the screen was only partially saved: the gates went to the Victoria and Albert Museum, but the remainder went for scrap.[9]

In *The Times* report, the Canon Treasurer explained that removal of the screen was part of an effort to return the cathedral to its original design and that 'the Chapter House renovations had been urgently needed and had meant the removal of glass which was of no artistic value'.[10] The Canon Treasurer was R S Dawson, a man with views (as we have seen from his comments in May 1964) about Victorian restorations. He had been appointed in 1958 and had played a big part in the 1959/60 reordering. In 1963 John Seeley (Lord Mottistone, one of the architect partners) died, and his obituary appeared in *The Times*. A few days later, a note appeared under the heading 'R.S.D. writes' which included:

> A much lesser known sphere was his share in the recent alterations in Salisbury Cathedral. Called in to advise in 1959 he took a firm and courageous stand which resulted in a substantial reshaping of the sanctuary and choir. This work included the removal of the Scott reredos and the encaustic tiles throughout the area for which he substituted a pavement of natural Purbeck.

Given the mention of Salisbury, it is difficult to see how 'R.S.D' could be anyone other than R S Dawson. Mention of firmness and courage suggests that the substantial reshaping entailed a substantial fight. Canon Dawson was not shy of controversy, nor was he a man to mince words. In February 1966 he intervened in a row about the proposed removal of a screen from another cathedral, writing to *The Times*:

> I doubt whether the plea for retaining the Scott-Skidmore screen in Hereford cathedral will be greatly enhanced by the publication today of your photograph of it in all its depressing enormity ... this is a purely Victorian fabrication which was a mistake when it was put up and remains a mistake now ... Its spiky, blatant vulgarity is such that ... it effectually destroys any enjoyment in the architectural qualities of the Cathedral itself ... it was a debased fashion that put in these metal screens 100 years ago irrespective of their surroundings.[11]

He further suggested that such things were as out of place as the crinoline and that their appropriate home was a museum 'where they can be admired and studied by their devotees'. The Canon's 'ferocious vocabulary' drew a rebuke from Nikolaus Pevsner, who asked[12] whether it had not occurred to the Canon that 'this is just the sort of way a serious, sensitive man like William Morris felt about Georgian architecture' but now 'the Georgian style is universally appreciated'.

Returning to the glazing issue, all fell quiet after May 1965, it having been reported in April that most of the masonry repairs to the first window had been completed. Ominously, on 23 May 1966, the Dean told the Chapter of correspondence with the Royal Fine Arts Commission, and that a member of the Victorian Society had visited the Chapter House. On 1 June 1966 the Greater Chapter expressed strong support for the decision to replace the Victorian glass but noted with anxiety that the RFAC had 'expressed a contrary opinion' and that this might jeopardise the appeal for building funds which was about to be launched.[13] At this point, one canon broke ranks and expressed doubts about the substitution of clear glass.

In September 1966 the cathedral architect (Lawrence Bond) reported that the six remaining Victorian windows required attention in the very near future. After 100 years the wire ties, which fastened the leads to supporting bars, had corroded. The supporting bars themselves had rusted and cracked the stone mullions.[14] A decision was now needed on whether to preserve the existing glass, or to continue the initiative to replace it with clear. On 15 October 1966 the Chapter decided that this was a matter for the Greater Chapter, at which the diocesan bishop would be present.[15] There was a disagreement, however, as to whether Mr Bond should be invited to speak to his report, and it was only by the Dean's casting vote that he was to be admitted for part of the meeting only.

The Greater Chapter met on 3 November 1966 to discuss this single issue. Among the external advisors attending was Sir Hugh Casson, eminent architect and member of the Royal Fine Arts Commission. He had been Director of Architecture for the Festival of Britain.[16] Canon Dawson made a strong case for clear glass, arguing that it improved the working environment. There was much support for this: the Archdeacon of Sarum asked Sir Hugh if 'the effects on the minds of those required to attend functions in the Chapter House should be taken into account'. Sir Hugh replied that it was ' impossible to judge the psychological effect but if one had the privilege of working in a place that is a work of art, one must be prepared to put up with the disadvantages.' The reaction to his remark is not recorded, but the Archdeacon asked if the windows had any intrinsic artistic value. Sir Hugh said that their main value was in the context of the Chapter House. It soon emerged that the Cathedrals' Advisory Committee – a national body set up in 1950 to give 'guidance when questions involving the preservation or enrichment of cathedral churches arise'[17] – had expressed its opposition to the removal of the Victorian glass.

After lunch, the external advisors withdrew and the architect, Mr Bond, joined the meeting. In presenting his report, he estimated that the cost of preserving the Victorian scheme would be £50 more per window than using clear glass, and so was not significant. He considered that clear glass would detract from the architectural merit of the Chapter House (if his view had been known in advance, it would explain why there was opposition to his attending the meeting). In spite of this advice, it is clear that Canon Dawson was supported by most of the Chapter, although the Bishop was 'torn' in that he did not like to reject the advice of the Cathedrals' Advisory Committee. The Archdeacon of Sarum proposed that the use of clear glass should continue, and this proposal was adopted with only two votes against.[18]

Any hopes that this was the end of the matter were quickly dashed. As the local planning authority, Wiltshire County Council's power to intervene in the Cathedral's programme was limited. In fact, on 5 December the Dean reported that he had asked Wilts CC whether the reglazing would require planning permission, and had been told that it would not. However, on 23 December 1966, Major S V Christie-Miller, Chairman of Wilts CC, wrote to the Dean asking for a special meeting of the Chapter at which all interested parties would be represented.[19] This was arranged for 13 January 1967. In the meantime, a paper[20] was prepared summarising the advantages of clear glass quarries. They:

1. provided better light levels for Chapter House users
2. offered views of the sky and of other parts of the building (the Architects' Journal subsequently reported that Canon Dawson preferred 'God's bright sunlight' to 'claustrophobic gloom')
3. were a typical feature of 20th century buildings and so represented contemporary craftsmanship, as was the tradition of the cathedral.

The meeting on 13 January was attended by representatives of Wiltshire County Council, Salisbury City Council, the Royal Fine Arts Commission, the Society of Antiquaries, the Society for the Preservation of Ancient Buildings, the Art Workers Guild, the British Society of Master Glass Painters, and the Ministry of Housing and Local Government.[21] It was pointed out that clear glass would give too harsh a light, and that quarries would alter the overall appearance of the cathedral, but the Chapter was apparently minded to stick to its decision.

At this point the gloves came off. At a special Chapter meeting on 16 January, the Dean reported news from Major Christie Miller that the laymen on the Appeals Committee had said that neither they nor other influential helpers would continue to participate in the major fund raising campaign planned for 1967 unless the Chapter was prepared to accept the advice of the Cathedrals Advisory Committee. Further, an assurance was required that in future the CAC would be consulted before any important alterations were made in the Cathedral (there appears, incidentally, to be no record of this having been formally reported to any of the Wilts CC committees). Canon Dawson objected that the Chapter was being asked to pass resolutions under duress, but nevertheless a Greater Chapter meeting was called for 25 January.

In the atmosphere of secrecy that seems to have surrounded events since 1965, rumours were circulating. On 20 January, the 'Here and There' columnist of the *Salisbury Times* wrote:

> Something is happening in the cathedral – exactly what is difficult to say. All I know is that on Friday a top level meeting was called by the Chairman of the Wiltshire County Council and the Dean and that it was all about something to do with the windows in the Chapter House.[22]

The Chapter met again on 25 January. It considered that its original decision to introduce clear glass had been correct, but it did not wish to jeopardise the funding campaign.[23] Canon Dawson again objected that the Chapter was acting under duress, and felt unable to support any change in the reglazing policy. The Dean later paid tribute to Canon Dawson's commitment to the Cathedral. The Chapter met again that evening and passed the required resolutions that they would seek the advice of the CAC in the preparation of a scheme both for the six remaining windows and those which now had clear glass, and that the CAC would be consulted in future. Canon Dawson was absent from this meeting. On 27 January *The Times* reported that the Victorian windows would stay and that those now in clear glass 'would be designed to be in harmony with them'.

Canon Dawson now made his views public. His letter which appeared in the *Church Times* on 10 February alleged that the Cathedrals' Advisory Committee was biased in

The replacement east window as completed by the cathedral glaziers

favour of Victorian art. He repeated the claim in an extensive interview with the chief reporter of the *Salisbury Times* published on the same day. He went further, saying that there was very powerful opposition from Victorian pressure groups, especially in Salisbury. However, he denied that he was an opponent of Victoriana but he wanted the Chapter House to be 'a place of beauty, not of drab, monotonous glass.'[24] He wrote to the *Salisbury Journal* saying that the work of contemporary craftsmen was being destroyed and that the decision was being taken in unreasonable haste.[25] This plea might have sounded strange considering how quickly the first two windows had been removed in 1965, but he could point out that one of them had fallen out over the Clerk of Works' staff.[26]

The *Salisbury Times* quoted a response from Mr W J Croome, Chairman of the CAC, denying any partiality but saying that, while the Victorian period had produced dull as well as fine work, 'it was a period of such widespread activity in the building of new and the repair of old churches as had not been known in England since the 15th century, and that the best evidences of that activity ought not to be expunged without trace from our great churches'.[27]

This appears to have marked the end of Canon Dawson's campaign. Plans were made for a reinstatement, releading and repair programme to be carried out by the cathedral's own glaziers but this did not start until 1970[28] because priority had to be given to spire repairs. Some windows were exchanged to balance the colours and patterns. First, the south and southeast windows were swapped. In 1978 the original east window was moved to replace the plain glass installed in the southwest in 1965. Work then started on a new east window, incorporating panels celebrating the National Farmers Union and the armed services nursing organisations and the General Nursing Council. The new window required the cutting, painting and firing of some 10,000 separate pieces of glass.[29] To this day, the west window (above the entrance) still comprises glass quarries. Sadly, Canon Dawson died in 1968.

Was there any wider significance in this dispute? Its most striking aspect was the freedom which Cathedral authorities enjoyed to alter historic buildings. There was a national advisory body, but it had no power to ensure that its advice was taken. The 'Canon of Barchester' article in the *Architects' Journal* bewailed the 'prevailing irresponsibility' of deans and chapters exemplified by the proposal to remove the Hereford screen. This was picked up by the *Church Times* the following day (10 February 1967 – the same edition that carried the Canon's letter alleging bias) and linked to the Salisbury dispute. On 9 February, Lord Amulree asked a question in the Lords as to 'whether it is the law of the land that a cathedral chapter can effect alterations to the fabric of their cathedral without reference to such advisory bodies as exist.' A government spokesman replied that there was no legal obligation to consult

Detail of the east window panel commemorating the centenary of the National Farmers' Union.
Photograph by Roger Ayres.

the Cathedrals' Advisory Committee but that 'the CAC are coming to see me in a week or two to review the way the present system works'.[30] Eventually, consultation was formalised in the Care of Cathedrals Measure 1990, but in 1967 it took a blunt threat about funding to change the Salisbury Chapter's mind.

Secondly, at a distance of some 50 years, it is difficult to recall the depth of the division between those who championed Victorian art and those who detested it as a monstrosity. This was exemplified locally on 21 April 1959 when *The Times* printed a photograph of the interior of Salisbury Cathedral after the Scott/Skidmore screen had been removed. Two letters appeared on 28 April. One of them said:

> ... you report the destruction of the great screen at Salisbury. Is it not a pity that those in charge of our greater churches seem to be about a generation behind in architectural appreciation? ... In a sense, of course, the Victorians are getting what they deserve since they destroyed so much fine work of the 18th century ....[31]

And the other:

Your lovely photograph of Salisbury Cathedral shows how much it has been improved by the removal of the choir screen. I hope that it will not be long before the ugly reredos also disappears.[32]

Canon Dawson was therefore far from alone in his attitude. However, by the time of the glazing dispute, popular perceptions were beginning to change. Victorian revivalists had never fallen completely silent and the voices of John Betjeman and Nikolaus Pevsner were increasingly being heard. Taste had apparently gone through a cycle:

It seems to be a law of our minds that we find the art forms of our fathers hideous, the art forms of our grandfathers amusing and those of our great-grandfathers attractive and even beautiful.[33]

Lastly, the 1960s were in some ways the heroic age of modern cathedral building. Coventry was consecrated in 1962 and Liverpool Metropolitan in 1967. Although building had started before World War II, Guildford – perhaps the most 'traditional' of the new cathedrals – was consecrated in 1961.[34] In the face of hostility towards perceived modernism, architects tried to define what the English tradition was. Describing visits to English medieval churches, Sir Basil Spence (the architect of Coventry Cathedral) said:

I realised too that in these churches was embodied a great truth: that architecture should grow out of the conditions of the time, should not be a copy of past styles, and must be a clear expression of contemporary thought. This I saw as our heritage, for we are an inventive nation and it is a denial of a natural characteristic to limit our architectural vocabulary to past forms ... Many sincere people, little realising that our tradition is such an adventurous one, are shocked when architects think in this traditional way; they cannot see that the true traditionalists are people who think simply in their own era. The copyists, then, are surely the revolutionaries.[35]

A further example is Liverpool Metropolitan. To many, this building would probably seem to owe little to the Gothic past. Yet even here its architect argued that he was innovating within a tradition:

In the atmosphere of Liverpool there is little of the bright sun and hard, clear light that made possible the precision of form and silhouette of the classic architecture of Greece and Rome. The atmosphere tends to be diffused and ethereal; the sun, if it appears at all, struggles through a haze of clouds. It has always seemed to me that the spiky silhouette of the Gothic cathedral mingles perfectly with the atmosphere of the Gothic North; rather than leave the tower as a rigid geometric form I diffused the silhouette by a structure of pinnacles.[36]

Canon Dawson's cause was probably not helped by his choice of words, but he was keen to ensure that the Chapter House was kept as a working environment (at one point the Chapter considering equipping it for meetings[37]) and was against 'shackling this magnificent building to a Victorian image for another 150 years'.[38] He was also determined to allow craftsmen to make a distinctive contemporary contribution to the building. In those respects he could have claimed to share the vision of the Coventry and Liverpool architects. Sir Basil Spence certainly had little time for stereotypical Victorian glass:

> I have seen very little stained glass in this country that had excited me. The sort of thing going into our great cathedrals and Westminster shocked me to the core. The true English tradition of stained glass can be seen at Fairford, Winchester, York and other places that have old glass of the thirteenth, fourteenth and fifteenth centuries. It is virile and strong; none of this wishy-washy stuff with sweet faces and poor realistic drawing.[39]

The Chapter House glass cannot be characterised in this way – apart from the stylised depictions of kings and bishops which surmount the windows, it is not representational. The main objections to it were its 'repetitiveness' and that it was oppressive. Whether or not this latter point was true in 1960s, it is difficult to say. It is hardly so now, especially on a sunny day, when the windows throw patterns of coloured light onto the floor. Most visitors nowadays would probably think that the Chapter House would be the poorer without its Victorian glass. Certainly, when told this story, they find it difficult to believe that anyone ever wanted to destroy the windows.

Acknowledgements

Special thanks are due to the Canon Chancellor, the Reverend Edward Probert, for making space in his busy schedule to let me see the Chapter papers. I am grateful to Roger Ayers for sharing with me his insights into what happened to the original 13th century glass, and into the patterns of the Victorian glass. Thanks also to Helen Taylor of the Wiltshire and Swindon History Centre and (as ever) to the staff of Salisbury Local Studies Library

.

Keith Blake worked as an administrator in the London Fire Brigade for more than 40 years. Retired, he is now a guide in the chapter house at Salisbury Cathedral and is interested in all aspects of the city's history.

[Ed. As Sarum Chronicle goes to press the Chapter House windows are being restored and maintained in a programme spanning14 months and costing £96000. This includes extensive releading, replacement of support bars and stonework restoration. Interior work should be completed by the end of 2012 and exterior work during 2013. The work should ensure that the glazing is in a good condition for the next 80-100 years.]

Bibliography

Blum, Pamela Z, 1998, *The Salisbury Chapter House and its 60 Old Testament scenes*, New Haven

Brown, Sarah, 1999, *Sumptuous and Richly Adorn'd*, RCHME

Burton, Anthony, 2004, *Victorian Decorative Art'* in Taylor, Miles and Wolff, Michael (eds), The Victorians since 1901, Manchester University Press

Chapter minutes held by the Cathedral library

Friends of Salisbury Cathedral, various years, *Spire*, annual reports of the Friends

Gibberd, Sir Frederick, 1968, *Metropolitan Cathedral of Christ the King, Liverpool*, The Architectural Press

Oxford Dictionary of National Biography (ODNB)

Richards, David, 2011, Reflections on medieval society: heraldic glass in Salisbury Cathedral –*Sarum Chronicle* issue 11, pp5-13

Salisbury appeal trustees, *Salisbury Cathedral Appeal 1967*, (booklet)

Spence, Sir Basil, 1962, *Phoenix at Coventry*, Geoffrey Bles

Spring, Roy, 1973, *The Stained Glass of Salisbury Cathedral*, Friends of Salisbury Cathedral

Tatton-Brown, Tim and Crook, John, 2009, *Salisbury Cathedral, The making of a medieval masterpiece*, Scala Publishers Ltd

Abbreviations

SJ= Salisbury Journal   STM = Salisbury Times

Except where otherwise stated, pictures are by the author.

Notes

1   Blum, p83
2   Richards, pp5-13
3   Brown, p88
4   Chapter minutes 20 May 1964 and 9 August 1964
5   Letter 28 January 1967 to *The Times*
6   Article by Symonson, Anthony, *Architects' Journal*, 9 February 1967
7   Tatton-Brown and Crook, pp124-125
8   Brown, p53
9   Chapter minutes record the start of the search on 4 October 1959. It continued into 1960.
10   *The Times* 29 May 1965
11   letter to *The Times* 28 February 1966
12   *Ibid* 2 March 1966
13   The *Salisbury Cathedral Appeal 1967* said that a total of £188,000 was needed for building work, including £11,500 for the Chapter House.
14   Dean's letter to *The Times*, 28 January 1967
15   Chapter minute, 15 October 1966
16   ODNB Vol 10 p 499. The entry notes that 'Casson's willingness to appear as expert witness

for the demolition of historic buildings was seen by many as an opportunistic abuse of his reputation'. He would not therefore have necessarily opposed the removal of Victorian glass.

17   *The Times*, 13 March 1950

18   Chapter minute, 3 November 1966

19   Cathedral library collection

20   *Ibid*

21   *SJ*, 23 February 1967

22   The meeting had taken place at the White Hart Hotel, and the columnist had met Major Christie - Miller during the lunch break

23   Chapter minute 25 January 1967

24   The interview throws further light on Canon Dawson's part in the removal of the choir screen in 1959. At one point he says of the changes which had taken place since his arrival in 1958 'all these <u>except for the metal choir screen</u> arose either directly or indirectly from Lord Mottistone's work which is so generally approved today'. The words which I have underlined suggest that removal of the screen was the Canon's own idea.

25   *SJ* 16 February 1967

26   *STM* 17 February 1967

27   *Ibid*

28   Spring, p22

29   *Spire* 1978 p24

30   Hansard vol 279 cc 1472-3 HL debate 9 February 1967

31   R D Reid of Wells

32   S Davis of Norfolk Street WC2

33   James Laver of the Victoria and Albert Museum, quoted in Burton

34   Its architect, Sir Edward Maufe, had been a consultant in the 1959/60 reordering of the Salisbury sanctuary, and was mentioned by Canon Dawson in his interview of 10 February 1967.

35   Spence, p9. He, like Sir Hugh Casson, had worked on the Festival of Britain.

36   Gibberd, p46

37   Chapter minute 5 September 1966. *Salisbury Cathedral Appeal 1967* (see above) said (p7) 'the Dean and Chapter intend to make increasing use of the Chapter House as a centre for various activities covering a very wide range' but that work was needed to the structure.

38   *SJ* 26 February 1967

39   Spence, p50

The Anglo Saxon and Medieval Mints at Salisbury and Wilton

Jeremy Ludford

Coinage in Anglo-Saxon and medieval England consisted principally of precious metal, usually silver, made by a number of English mints. The currency often included some foreign coins and base metal tokens. In addition, there were sometimes individual promissory notes. This account centres only on coins. It was not until the reign of Eadgar, in around 950AD, that the mint name and that of the moneyer were put on coins as a general rule.[1] Eadgar also introduced a vast re-coinage as the money circulating at the time had been debased by clipping.[2]

Throughout the counties of England and Wales there were 102 attested mints and a further 10 whose locations are uncertain (excluding baronial mints in the reign of Stephen, of which Trowbridge is probably one).[3] Mints were distributed in centres of population and, in cases of emergency, in areas of refuge. The minting of coins was franchised out by the State and tax was collected on a shire basis. Weight standards varied on a shire to shire basis, within small limits. There were seven known mints and possibly one other, operating in Wiltshire at some time during the Anglo-Saxon and Norman periods (973-1154). The English silver used for minting in Wiltshire probably came from Combe Martin, North Devon and Bere Ferrers in West Devon. Foreign silver would have been obtained in exchange for English exports.[4] The State was not generally the main supplier of bullion for minting, private individuals often had their own silver minted into coin and some foreign coins were melted down and re-coined as English.

A borough, or a Lord, either lay or ecclesiastical, could enjoy the profits from the services of a moneyer or even possess the right of mintage. Profits belonged to the moneyer, most of whom had bought the privilege, but ecclesiastical mints were established and had existed since the middle of the 8th century at Canterbury, Durham and York under royal patronage, from which the profits passed to the Crown and the Church. The main centres for the production of coinage during this period were London, Canterbury, Lincoln, Winchester and York, which accounted for 50% of the 100,000 coins known to have survived in total. At the other end of the scale, only about 25 coins are known from the Bedwyn mint.

Salisbury and Wilton were the main mints operating in Wiltshire. Salisbury was in production from the reign of Aethelred II (979-1016) until the reign of Henry II (1154-1189). Wilton was producing coins from the reign of Eadgar (959-975) until that of Henry III in about 1272. The mint name for Wilton appears as Pilt, Piltu or Piltune ('P' at that time was our 'W' hence 'Pince' for Winchester), Salisbury appears as Sereb, Saleb or Saerb.[5] Wilton was the more important of the two.

In the late Anglo-Saxon period and throughout Norman England, there were large numbers of moneyers in dozens of towns and cities. Boroughs were expected to have moneyers and minting was not allowed outside their boroughs. Because of a lack of written history, most of the moneyers are only known to us by their coins. Some useful information can be gathered from the Winchester Survey[6] which shows that moneyers were of burgess rank or otherwise people with land or property. Winchester had several mints, in the high street, usually associated with a forge. There is evidence that someone with the means could set up as a moneyer within a borough and buy the dies to mint coins. There does not seem to have been a very rigorous vetting procedure in place.

Moneyers could, however, operate in a number of boroughs, simultaneously. One moneyer, Wesinge, (who possibly came from Wilton[7] and was known to have travelled

Aethelred II penny by Saewine of Wilton (private collection)

Harold II penny by Alfwold of Wilton (private collection)

with King Aethelred II to Thetford, Norfolk, and to have minted coins there) appears to have produced coins in a number of areas, perhaps when travelling with the King at the time. Particularly after the year 1100 there is evidence of moneyers working in a number of boroughs. Tovi[8] was an itinerant moneyer who was known to have operated in London, Oxford, Winchester and Twynham (Christchurch) over a short period in time but others seemed to have worked in one place for up to 30 years.

Salisbury's mint at Old Sarum had six moneyers producing coins for Aethelred II (979-1016), whereas Wilton, in the same period, had eleven. (Malmesbury had three, Warminster two, Cricklade one and Bedwyn none during that time.) By the reign of Harthacnut (1035-1042), Salisbury had twelve, Malmesbury four and Wilton had six .[9] In the brief reign of Harold II – 9 January to 14 October 1066 – Wilton had fourteen and Salisbury had seven (the other Wiltshire mints had nine between them.)

Under the Normans, a new mint opened at Marlborough in the reign of William I (1066-1087) and Warminster closed. Bedwyn had one moneyer, Cilda, who also worked at Marlborough. The other mints in Wiltshire had between three and five moneyers each. By the time of Stephen (1135-1154), apart from Salisbury and Wilton, the other mints were only producing on an irregular basis.[10]

The minting of coins was first described in any detail c1247-1278, although it can be assumed that little had changed for many years prior to that. There are very few written sources about coin-making prior to the mid-13th century. Each monarch had several different styles of coin and each moneyer had a preference as to the style that he chose to produce.

A sample of molten metal bullion and alloy was mixed to a standard of fineness which was the sterling standard of 92.5% silver. A sample was taken from the middle of the pot and, if the assayer stated that it was up to standard, the content of the whole pot was poured into grooves in iron bars. These cast strips were reheated and quenched in water to anneal them. They were then hammered flat and cut with shears into coin blanks and checked for weight.[11] The weight of a silver penny would be between 0.9 and 1.5g. The blanks were then blanched to improve their appearance by boiling in Argol (tartar from wine casks). The coin blanks and the shearings were returned to the master for checking that there had been no loss, or theft, of precious metal. The penalties for theft, short weight or debased metal were severe. In 1124, Henry I summoned 94 moneyers to Winchester for issuing sub-standard coinage. Their punishment was to have one hand and one testicle removed.[12]

Coins were made by using a pair of dies.[13] The lower die was secured in a large block of wood, a disc of metal was placed on the lower die, the upper die placed above it and then given a hard hammer blow. The pairs of dies from which the coins were produced lasted about six years, with the upper die usually wearing out first. Dies were produced in a number of styles nationally and small regional variations can be detected. These slight differences can sometimes be compared and suggest that the top and lower dies became mixed up so a 'mule' coin was produced. The obverse of the coins, with the King's head, was of standard type but the reverse, where the mint and moneyer's name appeared, made the coins individual to that mint and moneyer. It is likely that the obverse dies might have been passed on if a mint closed down. Very few mints were in full production all the time, as production was dependent on the amount of bullion available in an area at any given time. Winchester was generally the centre for the production of dies for the region, although sometimes they were obtained from Exeter. As the dies carried the name of the mint and of the moneyer, there was a frequent need for replacement.

The changes in design were fiscal but the moneyers had to pay for their dies, usually 20 shillings and after a short interval a further 20 shillings to the King or the mint proprietor, as they were self-employed and sub-contracted workers. The Crown could claim fines for the use of an obsolete die which should have been defaced and returned to the Exchequer.

Coin design was varied nationally every six years or so until about 1035 when this change occurred every couple of years. Thus re-coinage occurred relatively frequently and coins can be dated to within a few years as a result of this. Dates on English coins did not appear until the 1550s.

Moneyers at work, drawing by Dr Jeanette Cayley

The other Wiltshire mints to produce coins included Malmesbury (appearing on coins as Mald, Mealdmes or Melme), which operated from the reign of Eadgar until the Norman Conquest. The known moneyers there included Wulfric, Leofget and Ealdred. The production from Malmesbury was small, but regular. Warminster (which appears as Porime) also minted coins from the reign of Eadgar until the reign of Edward the Confessor. Moneyers known to have worked there included Alfwold, Leofsige and Wolfstan. Cricklade (Crocgl, Creccelad or Cric) issued coins from the reign of Aethelred, in 979, until and including the brief reign of Harold II in 1066. Marlborough (Maerlemi) operated a mint from the conquest until the death of William II (Rufus) in 1100.[14] Bedwyn's (Bedepin) coinage was only produced under Edward the Confessor from 1042 to 1066. A moneyer there was called Cilda (Cild). The mint signatures were often abbreviated and spelling was no more reliable than that of other ages.

It is likely that some of the smaller mints only operated spasmodically as the need for coin occurred. Production varied from time to time. For example in the reign of Aethelred it was eight times higher than in Edward the Confessor's. There is some evidence that coins were minted at Trowbridge during 'The Anarchy' in the period from 1135-1154 when Stephen, Matilda and several barons issued coins. Matilda's coins were minted at Oxford, Bristol, Wareham and Cardiff, probably in 1141, following Stephen's defeat at the Battle of Lincoln and his subsequent imprisonment.[15] Matilda had effectively been Queen from 9 February. She probably spent the Easter of 1141 in Wilton, as Queen. However, Stephen had regained control of England by the end of the year.

There was an agreement that Matilda's son should become King upon Stephen's death. There are a small number of Matilda coins in existence and even fewer bearing the names of Brian Fitzcount, Henry de Neuberg and Earl Patrick of Salisbury.[16] An interesting hoard of these coins was found at Box in Wiltshire in 2004, when coins of Earl Robert of Gloucester and Earl William of Gloucester were discovered for the first time. Some of these baronial issues may have been minted at Trowbridge.

As coins bore the moneyer's name, those made during this period were often poorly produced. The moneyers were loath to declare their allegiance and during times of unrest they often blundered the legends on the coin so that their names were illegible.

Wilton, the major mint of Wiltshire, and Salisbury produced a large number of coins over a period nearly 300 years. In the short reign of Harold II a relatively large number of coins were minted at Wilton, which had suffered a setback when it was sacked in 1003 by Swein.[17] Salisbury (Old Sarum) became a refuge for the moneyers of the time and it is possible to trace the die types being used in Wilton then later in Salisbury. Harold's family had associations with Wilton. After his death, his sister Edith, who was Edward the Confessor's widow, lived in Wilton. She founded a nunnery and was later buried there.[18]

Huge numbers of coins were accumulated as the penny was usually the only coin. (In those days a penny a day was the standard wage.) Cash seized by Stephen at Winchester in 1135 comprised £100,000 (24 million pence) and when Bishop Roger stacked the residue of his fortune on the high altar of Salisbury Cathedral as a gift towards its completion it amounted to 80,000 marks (a mark was 13s 4d, a widely-used unit of account), over 12 million coins which would have weighed nearly 12 tons.[19] These vast mintages have long been melted down. The largest quantity of Norman coins so far found, including a number from Salisbury, was the Beaworth hoard found in 1833 near Winchester amounting to 8,000 coins, mostly from the reign of William I.[20]

In Henry II's reign, there were two moneyers at Salisbury, Daniel and Levric, and three in Wilton, Anschetil, Lantier and Willem. The Salisbury mint closed during Henry II's reign, when a new coinage – known as Short Cross coinage – replaced the 'Tealby' issue from 1180 onwards. In Henry III's reign, Huge Ion and Willem were the last moneyers to mint coins in Wiltshire.[21]

Henry III, who had been on the throne since 1216 and had been involved in the building of Salisbury Cathedral, was succeeded by Edward I (1272-1307) who set about a re-coinage in 1279 and issued a new denomination, the groat, worth four pence. Until this time, the denomination was almost solely the silver penny, which was frequently

cm

Edward the Confessor penny by Godric of Salisbury (private collection)

cut in halves and quarters to provide half-pennies and farthings. It is thought that this was often carried out at the mint using a chisel on a block. Halved pennies were often reckoned at three to the penny, making the shopkeeper a potential profit. There were also round farthings and halfpennies produced under most Saxon and Norman kings. Very few have survived, but a number have been found recently by the use of metal detectors. A round halfpenny of Eadgar, found as recently as September 2011 near Salisbury, was minted in Wilton by Boiga. Previously, round halfpennies of Eadgar were only known to have been struck at London, Winchester and Chichester.

Minting became centralised just as the last of the Wiltshire mints were closing, 1154-1180. This left only four mints – London, Canterbury, Bury St Edmunds and Durham. There was collective dismissal of nearly all the moneyers at that time. It was over 250 years later, in the reign of Edward III, before other English mints opened at Bristol, Coventry and Norwich.

Acknowledgements

I wish to thank the staff of the coin department at The British Museum for their help in locating relevant sources for this paper from their vast library, David Cousins for photographing the coins and Jeanette Cayley for creating the sketch of moneyers at work.

Jeremy Ludford is a retired Dental Surgeon, who qualified from Guys Hospital Medical School in 1969. He has family connections in Wiltshire back to at least the 17th Century. He has a keen interest in history, particularly Anglo-Saxon, Norman and Tudor periods.

Bibliography

Allen, Martin, 2012, *Mints and Money in Medieval England*, Cambridge University Press

Blunt, C E and Lyon, C S S, 1953, Some notes on the mints of Salisbury and Wilton, from Jonsson, K, (ed), 1990, *Studies in late Anglo-Saxon Coinage*, Numismatiska Meddelanden 35, Svenska numismatiska föreningen, pp25-34

Boon, George C, 1988, *Coins of the Anarchy.* National Museum of Wales in association with A H Baldwin & Sons Ltd

Cooper, Denis R, 1988, *The Art and Craft of Coinmaking*, Spink

Metcalf, D M, 1998, *An atlas of Anglo-Saxon and Norman Coin Finds, c973-1086*, Spink

North, J J, 1994, *English Hammered Coinage*, vol.1, 3rd edition, Spink

Pain, Nesta, 1978, *Empress Matilda. Uncrowned Queen of England*, Weidenfeld & Nicholson.

Shortt, H de S, 1948 (a), 'The Mints of Wiltshire: from Eadgar to Henry III', *Archaeological Journal* 104, pp112-128 [should be read in conjuction with Shortt (b)]

Shortt, H de S, 1948 (b), 'The Mints of Wiltshire', *Numismatic Chronicle,* 6th series, Volume 8, pp169-187

Skingley, Phillip, (ed), 2012, *Coins of England & the United Kingdom*, 47th edition, Spink

Williams, Gareth, *Was Edith the Last Anglo-Saxon Monarch of England?* (in preparation)

Notes

1   Skingley, 136
2   clipping – snipping pieces off the edges of the coins
3   Skingley, 146
4   Allen, 246, 259
5   Blunt & Lyon, 27-34
6   Allen, 7
7   Allen, 94-6; North, 172-8
8   Allen, 4-5
9   North, 172-8
10   North, 203-6; Allen, 41-3
11   Cooper, 33-8
12   Allen, 27
13   Allen, 115-6 for this paragraph
14   Shortt, (a) and Shortt, (b) passim
15   Boon, 25 & Pain, 85-9
16   Skingley, 150-1
17   North, 245
18   Williams
19   Boon, 11
20   Metcalf, 189, 240
21   Shortt (a), 127-8

Past Editions

Sarum Chronicle was first published by the current editorial team in 2001. Many of the past editions are still available. The content of these earlier editions is listed below:

Issue 11: 2011

Reflections on medieval society: heraldic glass in Salisbury Cathedral
Origins of the Royal Society 1660 and the Wessex Connections
Bishop John Wordsworth 1843-1911
Community oral and public history in the Milford Street Bridge area of Salisbury
Sarum College and the Miss Wyndhams of the Close
Baptists in Shrewton: an initial foray
Salisbury Guildhall – renovated and revitalised
St Paul's Home Fisherton Anger and its founder
Salisbury's Assembly Rooms 1740–1960
Edward Thomas Stevens: Museums and education in mid-Victorian Salisbury
Screw Pump follow-up
Review: *New Directions in Local History since Hoskins*

Issue 10: 2010

Dr Roberts' Clock Tower
The Rise and Decline of Quakerism in South Wiltshire
Girl Guiding in the Salisbury area: some events from the first 60 years
Salisbury's Aesthetic Sunflowers
The Topp family of Coombe Bissett
Southampton's Brokage Books – their relevance to Salisbury
Celebrating 150 Years of Salisbury Museum

Issue 9: 2009

Anne Bodenham's trial for witchcraft in 1653
Dorothy Sayers at the Godolphin School
The spatial arrangements of chantry chapels in Salisbury Cathedral
Reconstructing the medieval Landscape around Salisbury
17th century Life and Strife at Salisbury Cathedral
Women's Suffrage Movement in Salisbury

Issue 8: 2008

Thomas Hardy and Salisbury
William Bird Brodie
Life and Death in Fisherton Gaol, 1800-1850
Early Maps of the Salisbury Countryside

Amesbury Carnivals in the 1920s
St Andrew's Church, Laverstock, 150th Anniversary
Richard Cockle Lucas, a Salisbury Sculptor
Salisbury: the seaport that never was

Issue 7: 2007

The Last Days of St Clement's Church, Fisherton Anger
Heale House and Harold Ainsworth Peto
College to Council House
Salisbury Head Post Office reaches its 100th birthday
Deconstructing Wilton
Wyndham Park: a late Victorian suburb
The Hall of John Hall's Victorian Facade

Issue 6: 2006

Preparations against invasion in the Salisbury area in1803
The Greencroft
Salisbury in the Age of Cholera
The Reverend Doctor John Baker of Salisbury
George Herbert's Bemerton
The 1906 Salisbury Railway Disaster
Salisbury and the Religious Census of 1851
John Frederick Smerdon Stone

Issue 5: 2005

Salisbury Cathedral's Tower and Spire
Economic activity in the Wardour Woods
Housekeeping in Salisbury, 1640
Music in late Victorian Salisbury
Recipients of the Freedom of Salisbury
Handel's Messiah: the Salisbury connection
Trafalgar: some Salisbury connections

Issue 4: 2004

Fisherton Anger (Salisbury Devizes Road) Cemetery Pt 2
The Treasury and Muniment Room at Salisbury Cathedral
Where was Old Sarum?
The Spinster and the Plague
William Butterfield and the restoration of St Mary's Church, Dinton
Salisbury as a seaport: some further debate
Mathematical tiles in Salisbury
The 150th anniversary of the Charge of the Light Brigade

Past Editions

Issue 3: 2003

Henry Fawcett, 1833-1884
Community policing in late medieval Salisbury
J Arthur Reeve and St Mark's Church
Salisbury as a seaport
'Saved to serve': fallen women in Salisbury
A theatre fit for the new millennium
Bishopdown: the missing links

Issue 2: 2002

The First World War and its impact on Salisbury
17th century farming in the Salisbury district
Salisbury's provincial 'Great Exhibition'
Salisbury under the later Stuarts
Pugin, St Osmund and Salisbury
Salisbury's military museum - making history more accessible

Issue 1: 2001

The burning of Salisbury Council House
The Salisbury School Board
Mr Bristol's Academy
Hamstone in Salisbury
Lady Elizabeth Herbert of Lea
Fisherton Anger (Salisbury Devizes Road) Cemetery Pt 1
Dinton in the 16th Century
Making a Stonehenge Gallery